THE SMART ONE
A GRANDFATHER'S TALE

THE SMART ONE
A GRANDFATHER'S TALE

KEN GOODMAN

GARN PRESS
NEW YORK, NY

Published by Garn Press, LLC
New York, NY
www.garnpress.com

Copyright © 2015 by Kenneth S. Goodman

The Smart One: A Grandfather's Tale is a work of fiction. Where real-life historical and public figures appear, the situations, incidents, and dialogues concerning those persons are fictional interpretations. Other names, characters, places, and events are used fictitiously, and in all respects, any resemblance to real persons, living or dead, is entirely coincidental.

Garn Press and the Chapwoman logo are registered trademarks of Garn Press, LLC

All rights reserved. No part of this publication may be reproduced, distributed, or transmitted in any form or by any means, including photocopying, recording, or other electronic or mechanical methods, without the prior written permission of the publisher, except in the case of brief quotations embodied in critical reviews and certain other noncommercial uses permitted by copyright law. For permission requests, please send an email to Garn Press addressed "Attention: Permissions Coordinator," at *permissionscoordinator@garnpress.com*

Book and cover design by Ben James Taylor/Garn Press
Cover and book illustrations copyright © 2015 by Ray Martens

Library of Congress Control Number: 2015932587

Publisher's Cataloging-in-Publication Data

Goodman, Kenneth S.
 The smart one: a grandfather's tale / Kenneth Goodman.
   pages cm
 ISBN: 978-1-942146-10-0 (pbk.)
 ISBN: 978-1-942146-11-7 (hardcover)
 ISBN: 978-1-942146-09-4 (e-book)
 1. Jews—Social life and customs—Fiction. 2. Jewish children—Fiction. 3. Fasts and feasts—Judaism—Fiction. 4. Jews—Persecutions—Russia—Fiction. 5. Russia—History—Revolution, 1905-1907—Fiction. 6. Survival—Fiction. I. Martens, Ray, ill. II. Title.
PZ7.1.G66 Sm 2015
[Fic]—dc23
        2015932587

Table of Contents

Foreword	1
We're on Our Way: May 1906	4
Sukkos: October 1901	11
A Shabbos in 1902 When I Was Five	19
Chanukah: December 1903	27
Mixing in: The Strike on May Day, 1904	36
The Wedding: May 3, 1904	50
My First Whole Day Without Food: September 1904	65
Revolution in Smorgon: January 1905	79
The Kaziuk Fair and the Trial: March 1905	96
Purim and the Rescue: March 1905	115
Passover 1906 When I Was Nine	132
Goodbye Karka, Goodbye Smorgon: April 1906	148

Foreword

My father, Maxwell David Goodman, who was called Max, was born Duvid Mendel Gutman in Smorgon which is now in Belarus, a former Soviet Republic. At the time he lived there from his birth in 1897 to 1906 when he moved to Chicago, Smorgon was in the Vilnius (in Yiddish Vilna) district of Lithuania. Lithuania, at that time, was a part of the Russian empire. Smorgon was a shtetl, a small, mostly Jewish village that was evolving into an industrial town with a developing leather industry.

It had two claims to fame. It was the birthplace of the bagel (in Russian baronok). And it was home to the famous School for Bears which continued until World War I. The local noble family was the

Radziwills. Count Radziwill was the patron of the bear school. He also permitted a few Jewish families to farm some of his land and share their profits with him in the tiny community of Karka, just outside Smorgon.

That much is history. My father didn't talk much about his childhood. He was the youngest of five children and the only boy. He had four older sisters who ranged from 15 to 2 years older than him.

My intention in writing this book for young people is to show the events and conflicts in his young life and among the Jews who were migrating in large numbers to America at the turn of the 20th century. His childhood was a time of great change in Eastern Europe. Within his home there was conflict between the traditional religious views his parents represented and the "enlightened" revolutionary views and activities of his older sisters.

What I have created is a historical novel. The main characters in telling his story are his actual family members. I have stayed close to the events of their lives as I knew them. One exception is Kate's husband whom she did not actually meet until she moved to Chicago. I needed him in my story to bring the culture of the enlightenment into the family home. I have also taken great pains to stay true to actual historical events and their local manifestations. I visited Smorgon and was helped greatly by Valentina a local librarian and Nadya a museum curator. Svetlana Satalova of the Gaon National Jewish Museum in Vilnius was my guide and translated many original documents. The other characters in the novel are based on real people like those Duvid Mendel and his family would have known and interacted with.

My father and his family came to America as the result of complex and powerful events. They changed after coming to America.

But what they brought with them also changed America. To understand who we are as Americans we need to understand who we were and where we have been.

In America Max's father never found a place for himself. He died a few years after the move. His mother kept up the traditions and supported herself as she dedicated herself to her grandchildren. Max's sisters continued to work in the garment industry and were active in radical political and Yiddish cultural groups.

In America, Max rejected both religion and politics as he pursued but never achieved "The American Dream." The succeeding generations became writers, teachers, scholars, doctors. Some are religious, some not. Some are politically active, some not. And all of David Mendel (Max) Goodman's children, grandchildren and great grandchildren have been influenced by the events of his childhood in ways they may not know.

Ken Goodman
January, 2015

One
We're on Our Way: May 1906

Good news: We're finally on our way to America. It seems like all my life I've been dreaming about going to America.

Bad news: We're leaving the only place I've ever lived in my whole life. I thought that I would be happy to be on my way to America but now that I'm leaving I'm really sad.

Smorgon, the shtetl, the little town we're leaving, is famous for two things: bears and bagels. Bagels were invented in Smorgon and Smorgon bagels are sold at all the fairs in our part of the world. And there is a famous school for bears in Smorgon. In the woods around Smorgon there are lots of bears. But there are also wild strawberries, nuts and mushrooms that a smart kid can gather and sell in the market to get some money. I'm going to miss that. I wonder if they have woods in Chicago. Actually we lived in a tiny place called Karka just outside Smorgon. In Karka everybody but us are farmers. They brought Papa to be their Rabbi and to be a rebbe, a teacher of their little boys.

I dream a lot and up until now my dreams about going to America are mostly about getting rich in America. But just now as I was riding in the wagon with Papa, Mama and my sisters, Dvoira and Sarah on our way to take the train in Vilna I fell asleep. And I had this bad dream.

My sisters, Kate and Anna, were in the wagon with us which was already strange because I knew they were in Chicago waiting for us. Kate's married to Maish, who is also in Chicago. But in my dream he was driving the wagon. And instead of horses the wagon was being pulled by two bears. And instead of all the things we had packed to take with us to America, there was nothing but bagels in the wagon with us. We were up to our necks in rings of bagels.

In this strange dream Papa and my sisters were shouting at each other. That wasn't strange because Kate and Anna often argued with Papa. It was what they were saying that was strange. They were arguing about me.

"He's a smart boy. In America he will become a Rabbi like his Papa and his Papa's Papa and those that came before them," said Papa.

"No," said Kate. "He's a smart boy. In America he will join the movement and fight for freedom like us."

"He'll lead strikes," said Anna.

"He'll sing revolutionary songs," said Maish.

"Hurray for Duvid Mendel, the Smart One!" the bears sang out in perfect Yiddish.

Mama put her arms around me and sang me a Yiddish lullaby.

Unter Mendele's vigele
Shteyt a klor-vays tsigele

It was my favorite one about a baby goat that grows up to sell raisins and almonds.

"That's what my Duvid Mendel will be in America, a rabbi who also makes a good living selling things."

I wanted to tell them that I was going to be rich in America but when I spoke it was some strange language none of them could understand.

Sarah started poking me in the ribs and I woke up. "Duvid Mendel," she said, "stop making those funny noises."

What a dream!

So now we are sitting in the railway station in Vilna, Mama, Papa, Dvoira, Sarah and me waiting for the train that will take us to a place called Hamburg where we will get on a steamship to go to America. Except Papa is not sitting. He is walking back and forth muttering to himself, "America. The stones will be traif there."

I ask, "How can stones be unkosher?" Some people say the streets are paved with gold in America. Maybe gold is unkosher. But Papa just keeps muttering.

There is a train station in Smorgon and we could have come to Vilna by train. But the police watch the train station to see who comes and goes. So we left at night in a wagon.

"All these many years our family has lived here," said Papa, "and now we have to leave like thieves in the night."

For now my name is Duvid Mendel Gutman. I also have some other names. My family and my friends usually call me Duvidel, little Duvid. Sometimes when I act silly they call me Duvidka. And when I was little Mama and Papa called me tatela, which means little Papa in Yiddish. For a long time I thought tatela was my name. But my favorite name is Der Kliegele, the little smart one. Papa started calling me that when I began to learn to read Hebrew in his school. My sisters called me that in the beginning to make fun of me because I'm the baby in the family. But when they saw how smart I really am, they began to call me that all the time. My sister Dvoira says when I get to America I'll probably get a new name. Jewish names don't sound very good in English, she says.

I'm about nine years old. She's about 15. She also says we'll all need something called a birthday when we get to America. You can't do anything without a birthday in America. She asked Maish to figure out her American birthday. Maish was a Yeshiva student and knows about such things. Dvoira knew she was born ten days before Pesach in 1891. He also figured out a birthday for my sister, Sarale, who is two years older than me. But I've decided that my birthday will be whatever day we get to America. Dvoira says it will be a chance for a new life in a new country, so I decided my birthday will be the first day in America.

I want to remember Karka and Smorgon so I've been writing things down in this notebook. I want to remember the good times I had with my family and friends and I don't want to forget the bad things. There were so many bad things that happened, really bad things. That's why we're leaving. But there were good times too.

The boss of all of Russia is a man called the Czar who lives far away in a city called St Petersburg. Maish taught me a song about the Czar. I only know the chorus:

> *Czar Nikolai*
> *Oh what a guy*
> *We'll all get together*
> *And punch him in the eye!*

Kate and Maish and Anna laughed when I sang that song but they wouldn't teach me the verses. They say I can only learn them when I get older. I think they say something about the Czar's wife or his mother. Papa got very angry when he heard me sing it. He yelled at Kate and Anna: "Why do you teach the boy to sing dangerous songs?"

Papa says hundreds of years our people lived here and mostly the Christians left us to our own ways as long as we stayed to ourselves. Now Jews are mixing into the politics of the gentiles and we have to leave.

"But it's a new day," says Dvoira. "If we get rid of the Czar and the bosses who oppress us, it won't matter who is Jew and who is gentile. We'll be citizens of Russia." Dvoira liked to use big words like oppress.

I have never been to a regular school. There are some schools in Smorgon but only the goyim – Christians - get to go to them. When I was very little, I would sit in the corner when Papa was teaching. He was surprised when I began to read Hebrew. So then I became part of his class.

I'm writing in Yiddish but I use the Hebrew letters I learned from Papa. Yiddish is the language we Jews around here speak.

Nobody taught me to read and write Yiddish. Yiddish isn't like Hebrew at all; it's more like German. Anna says Hebrew is only for study of musty old books and praying. That makes Papa very angry. "We must learn to read and write Hebrew to know how to live our lives. Otherwise we'll forget we are Jews."

Whenever I ask Papa why we do things the way we do, he always responds the same way. "That's the way it is written! Study hard, my yingele, my young one, and you will know how to live a good life full of mitzvahs, blessings."

Kate says, "We all will study, boys and girls too. Then we will make a new life for ourselves." I like to listen to them. But I don't like the shouting.

I learned to read Yiddish from the Yiddish books and newspapers Kate and Anna brought to the house before they went to America. That pleased them and they would answer my questions when I wanted to make sense of something. They never went to any real school but when they went to work in Smorgon they joined the Movement. In the Movement they have a system. Every member who knows something teaches it to the others. The students teach the workers and workers teach each other. And so Kate and Anna learned to read and write Yiddish and some Russian from the students. Kate took me with her some times to the workers' library where the Bund, the Jewish union, brings books for its members and their friends to read.

And so now I can read and write Yiddish and Hebrew. And Dvoira has even shown me how to read the letters that are in the Russian signs in Smorgon. Anna sent a little paper book they use in schools in America. Wouldn't you know? They don't use either Russian or Hebrew letters in the schools in America. On the boat I'm going to figure out how to read English. Even Jews can go to school in America. I can't wait. What's the good of being smart if you can't go to school?

I got a little bit involved in some of Kate and Anna's movement things and that made Papa angry and worried. Twice I even had the police chasing me. So Papa has been keeping me busy with extra lessons everyday so that I can read the Torah. He said that I will go to the Yeshiva when I am old enough.

I said, "But Papa you have no money."

"They'll have to make room for a smart boy. Besides you're the son of Reb Yankle Laib, the son of Reb Duvid Mendel, the son of Reb ItzakYosef," he said. Papa is very proud that his father and his father's father were also rabbis. He thinks I will be a rabbi too. But in America anyone who is smart can be rich. So why I should I be a rabbi and be poor like Papa?

Two
Sukkos: October 1901

Until I was four, my favorite Yom Tov was Sukkos. On Sukkos all the Jews in Karka built open shelters called sukkahs with tree branches for a roof. Papa says that a long, long time ago, when Jews all lived in Judea, the Jews would build shelters in the fields to sleep in when they picked their crops. In Karka, it was too cold to sleep there, but for eight days our family ate our meals in our sukkah. The Jewish farmers in Karka have to share what they grow with Count Radziwill who owns the land and lets them farm it. But for Sukkos there is usually plenty to eat. And the trees are loaded with apples, pears, plums and cherries.

At the end of Sukkos there is a big celebration. Every day of the year a short part of the Torah is read in the synagogue. The last part is read on the last day of Sukkos which is called Simchas Torah. That night we take the Torah from a box that hangs on the wall. It has doors that open so we can take out the Torah to read the day's portion. My Papa, the rabbi, carries it and we all follow, singing. We follow the rabbi out of the synagogue and around the outside of the synagogue in a parade carrying apples with lighted candles and flags in the middle. We sing special songs as we march around.

One reason I liked the high holidays is that Kate and Anna got to come home from their jobs in Smorgon. Kate worked in a factory knitting socks and Anna worked in a bagel bakery. Sometimes Anna would bring home some left over bagels and Mama would warm them in the oven and we'd have them with butter or cheese and a glass of milk for a meal.

Mama worked selling milk that she would get from the farmers in Karka. She carried a yoke on her shoulders with a bucket of milk on each side which she sold by the dipper to the people who lived in Smorgon. Dvoira says that the day after I was born my mother was back selling her milk. Sometimes I would go with Mama to help her and to see my friends in Smorgon.

The meal we had in our sukkah on that last day of Sukkos in 1901 was wonderful. Papa didn't make much money teaching little boys and being the Rabbi for the farmers in our little village. But sometimes, especially on holidays, the farmers would pay Papa with some potatoes or a few eggs. Papa also knew the kosher way to kill chickens and the prayers to say when you kill them and he would do that for our neighbors. Then they would give him a chicken. I think maybe it was an old hen that stopped laying eggs.

So at our dinner that night Mama made chicken soup with homemade noodles. I was always afraid to watch her make the noodles. She'd mix the eggs and flour and then roll out a very thin sheet. Next she'd roll the sheet into a tight roll. Then came the scary part. She'd sharpen her knife and then - snip, snip, snip, snip. Snip - she'd move one hand along the roll chopping off perfect thin noodle rolls with the knife in the other hand so fast I was sure she was going to cut herself, but she never did. Then it was my job to hang the noodles over the backs of chairs to let them dry before they were boiled for the soup.

After the soup we all had a piece of chicken. Mama always ate the feet. She said she liked them best. I got the pupik. People have pupiks, belly buttons. But the chicken's pupik is some place inside it. Sometimes we'd find eggs in the chicken, just the yolks in a string each a bit larger than the next. Those were boiled in the soup and the girls got to eat them. The eggs would make them fertile, Mama said, so they could have children someday. For a special treat Mama would cut off the neck skin and sew it at one end. She would stuff the neck skin with a stuffing made from flour, onion and chicken fat. Then she'd sew the other end and boil the helzel, the stuffed neck skin, in the soup. It tasted so good!

We finished our dinner and the kids from Karka began to arrive with their apples and candles for the Simchas Torah parade. The men of Karka would sometimes go into Smorgon to a big synagogue for the other high holidays but for Simchas Torah the prayer house next to our house was the shul. Papa had a Torah which was his father's and his father's father's. Being the only boy I was named for my Zaide, my grandfather, who died before I was born.

Just as we were lighting the candles for the parade Maish and some of the other young men came running. They were shouting "The Cossacks are coming! The Cossacks are coming!" Even when I was that little I knew the Cossacks were terrible. They came riding horses and waving their terrible swords. "They're arresting Union members and people from the Movement. We've got to hide in the woods."

Already we could hear the galloping horses in the distance.

Kate and Anna quickly gathered their things and ran with the young men and women toward the woods. Papa picked up the Torah and told the children to follow him and start marching and singing. Some of them had started crying but as we started our march they stopped and started singing.

The Cossacks rode their horses into and over our sukkah knocking over everything. The leader leaned down from his horse and shouted something in Russian to Papa who kept on walking and singing. He took the tip of his sword and knocked the Torah from Papa's hands. Papa picked it up and said to us children in Yiddish, "Keep marching and singing." Then he said something to the Cossack leader in Russian.

The Cossack said, "Jew, tell us where the union people are."

Papa said, "We are all poor farmers here, tenants of Count Radziwill. Our crops and our houses belong to the Count. If you destroy them, you'll have to answer to him."

The Cossacks had already set fire to one of the fields, but their leader called to them to stop. Then he let two of his men ride their horses through our sukkah and right into the house breaking dishes and furniture. Now our wonderful day was a terrible day.

The Cossacks turned their horses toward the woods. But Dvoira, in what Russian she could manage, called out, "Watch out for the bears. Don't you know about the famous Smorgon bears? The woods are full of them."

"She's right," said Mama. "There is even a famous school in Smorgon for training bears." Everyone in fact knew about the bears of Smorgon. The Cossacks remembered the bears too.

And then, as fast as they came, the Cossacks were gone back toward Smorgon. After they got the fire in the field out, the men of Karka came to help us straighten up and to have a drink of schnappes with Papa. The schnappes is only for grown-ups. I asked Papa why it's OK to drink on Simchas Torah and he said, "Azoi iz geschriebn." So it is written. That's how he always answered.

Much later Kate and Anna and their friends came quietly out of the woods.

"Did the bears hurt you?" I asked.

"We have a secret place in those woods where we hold our meetings," said Anna. "We know how to scare the bears away with our torches."

"And we have a secret weapon," said Kate. "Avram, here works at the school for bears. He keeps two trained bears in the woods. If the Cossacks had followed us, you can be sure that our trained bears would have protected us."

I didn't know whether Kate was telling the truth or just making up a story but I had seen a bear pulling a wagon on a street in Smorgon so I didn't doubt Kate and Anna's friends could train bears to fight Cossacks.

"Your Papa is a hero," said Avram. "Let's drink a toast to our Rabbi who stood up to the Cossacks."

"L' Chaim, long life, Reb Yankle Laib," everyone shouted.

Papa had been a hero with the Cossacks. But now he became very angry.

"Kate, Anna why do you desert our traditions and belong to dangerous organizations. It's bad enough you have to work in Smorgon and not live at home with your family. But you are getting bad habits and even worse ideas from your friends. Jews have survived for centuries in this place by staying out of the fights of the gentiles. Our strength comes from our religion."

"Papa," said Anna. "This is a new time. A time of haskalah, of enlightenment. Jews can become citizens of their countries. They can join with other revolutionary people to get rid of our oppressors."

"Our friends are good people, Papa," said Kate. "They have helped us learn. They have helped us to see that women have rights too, that we don't have to work 15 hours a day for half a ruble."

"Times are changing, Reb Yankle Laib," said Kate's friend Maish. Maish was a student in the Yeshiva. "In the leather factories in Smorgon the workers work 15 hours a day. Papas never see their children. They start work long before the children are up and come home long after the children are asleep."

"Is that what you learn in the Yeshiva? And have they also taught you to disrespect your father. Your father owns a leather factory. Where in the Torah does it say a son may oppose his father?" Papa replied.

But before Kate or Anna or their friends could respond, Mama called out, "Enough already. We've had enough trouble to spoil our holiday."

Maish started to sing a new Yiddish song he knew Papa would like. "It's about you, Reb Yankle Laib." In Yiddish he called it Oifn Pripichek - a pripichek is the oven that is in the middle of the house where we cook. It keeps us warm and there's a ledge on top where Sarah and I get to sleep because we're small and the youngest.

In the fireplace a warming fire burns
And the house is hot
And the rebbe teaches ABC'S
To every eager tot.

Tell me little ones
Remember what you've learned,
What you're learning here.

Say it once again
and yet another time
The sounds the letters say.

Say it once again
And yet another time
The sounds the letters say

Maish learned the song from a man they called Chaver Warshavsky. He came to Smorgon to sing Yiddish songs he made up. Papa got really angry when he heard us singing a part of the bund anthem we heard Maish singing.

This was not the first time I had heard my father and my sisters argue and the arguments became part of my education. I knew they loved each other, though sometimes if you heard them shouting you'd have a hard time believing that. I knew my father was ashamed that my sisters had to work and not stay at home until they married. I knew he felt bad that he would not have money for them to get proper husbands. And I came to know that though he was respected and honored by our little village, he was troubled that things were changing all around him.

Mama took his side in these arguments. But she couldn't help be proud of her daughters, who sacrificed their own young years to work and bring money to the family. She kveled - took pleasure - in their leadership and they're good ideas, even if she didn't understand them. She was a strong woman herself, who kept all the traditions but worked to support her family and her scholar husband. But Mama knew better than any of us where all this was leading. And it was Mama who decided it was time for us to leave.

As for me, I learned to love the traditions. But it was my sisters' world that was exciting. And even then I knew that I would find my world in America. In America there were no limits for somebody smart like me.

Three

A Shabbos in 1902 When I Was Five

How I loved the way our family celebrated Shabbos, the Sabbath. Saturday is Shabbos, but it starts at sundown on Friday night. That makes Fridays special too. Here's how my day would be spent on Friday. Mama would get up before the sun came up and go to the farmers to get milk. When she'd come back, she'd get Sarale and me up to go with her to deliver her milk. Because Mama was working, from the time Dvoira was 10 or 11 it was her job to get the house ready for Shabbos.

On some Friday mornings, Mama would drop me at my friend Yussele's house in Smorgon. Yussele is some kind of a cousin. I think every Jew in Smorgon is every other Jew's cousin if you go back far enough. Yussele's family is Chassidic. They dress in black and do a lot of singing and dancing in their synagogue. They think their Rabbi has magic powers.

Maish taught me a song about a Chassidic Rabbi called Rabbi Elemelach. In the song the rabbi is enjoying some schnappes and gets very happy, and so he calls for his two fiddlers to fiddle. Then he gets happier and he calls for his two tooters to toot. Finally he is really happy and he calls for his two cymblars to cymbal. At the end of the song they're all playing at once.

> *Oh the rabbi Elemelach*
> *was becoming very happy*
> *was becoming very happy Elemelach*
> *So his hat he did doff*
> *and his coat he took off*
> *and he called for his fiddlers, the two.*
>
> *And the fiddlers they did fiddle,*
> *they did fiddle they did fiddle*
> *they did fiddle and did fiddle*
> *so did they.*
>
> *Yes the fiddlers they did fiddle*
> *they did fiddle they did fiddle*
> *They did fiddle and did fiddle,*
> *Oi vey!*

You get the idea, the same with the tooters and the cymblars. When I sang it for Yussele and his mother I thought they might be mad but they laughed and said there's nothing wrong with a happy rabbi who sings and dances when he prays.

Then Papa came for me and we went together to the shvitz bod, the steam bath. We need to make ourselves clean and put on our best clothes for the Sabbath. I love the steam bath. Kids like me sit on the lowest benches where it is not so hot but Papa climbs up to the top where there is a cloud of steam and it is very hot. We beat our skins with bundles of twigs. Then we put on our fresh clothes and walk home. Most of our neighbors are also coming home from the bath.

I liked it when Kate's friend Maish came to dinner Friday nights, and since he became Kate's special friend he was coming almost every Shabbos. His father is rich with his leather factory and Maish usually brought something special like a Challah, a twisted egg bread, which we ate on Shabbos instead of the usual black bread we had on other days.

Dinner Friday night is the most special meal of the week because it's the beginning of Shabbos.

Often it starts with gefilte fish. Mama buys the fish on the way home from delivering her milk. She carefully skins the whole fish and then takes the bones out. Then she chops up the raw fish and mixes it with eggs, a little matzo meal, chopped onions and salt and pepper. Then she makes egg-shaped balls of the chopped fish and wraps them in the fish skin. She boils the fish balls with the bones and carrots or celery if she can get some.

When the fish is done cooking, she strains the broth to get out the bones and cuts up the carrots to put on the plate with the fish balls. The broth turns to a kind of jelly which we eat with the fish.

Papa grinds up some horseradish to eat with the fish too. It took me a while to learn to like horseradish. The first time I ate it I took a big spoonful in my mouth. It burned my mouth and I got a really funny feeling up into my nose. Tears came into my eyes and my nose started running.

Now I like horseradish especially when Papa chops some beets with it and makes it bright red and sweeter. But I'm careful not to eat more than a little bit with some fish. Papa looks funny when he's grating the horse radish because tears run down his face and he's always blowing his nose in a big white handkerchief.

After the fish we have chicken soup with my mother's homemade noodles, chicken and potato kugel, another favorite of mine. Mama cooks the kugel in a heavy iron frying pan and puts chicken fat on top of the grated potatoes so it gets really crusty.

Saturday is the only day that Kate and Anna didn't work and I loved to hear them sing songs on Friday night and hear the stories they and their friends shared. Sarale and I hated to be away from them. So one Saturday afternoon we followed Kate and Anna and Dvoira when they went into the woods even though we knew we weren't supposed to go there. We knew there were bears but we remembered Kate said they could keep the bears away. We stayed close but tried to stay out of sight.

We followed them for a long time but then they went into some thick bushes and when we tried to follow them we couldn't find them. After a few minutes we got really scared. What if we don't find them and we can't find our way back ourselves? Sarah decided we should climb a tree to see if we could see them. That was a really good idea because just when we got up in the tree a bear came out of the woods. Maybe he smelled us because he came right up to the tree we were in. He put his front legs on the tree and looked right up at us, growling the whole time, and shaking his big head from side to side. We were afraid he would climb up the tree and get us.

And then a very strange thing happened. The bear began to talk to us in Yiddish! "Who told you you could come into my woods?" the bear said. "Don't you know that we bears can eat children who come into our woods?"

"But how is it you can talk in Yiddish, Mr. Bear?" I said.

"So how should I talk to you?" said the bear. "You wouldn't understand my bear language."

"But how is it that you can talk at all?" said Sarah.

"I've been to school," said the bear. "Didn't you know there's a famous school for bears in Smorgon? That's where I learned to speak Yiddish."

Just then we heard some laughing. "That's enough already, Avram," a voice said. It sounded like Anna. "You've got these children scared enough."

And suddenly there were my sisters and a lot of their friends under our tree looking up and laughing. When we climbed down, we were still a little worried about that bear.

"Is this one of the trained bears you said protected you?" said Sarah.

"Not exactly," said Kate.

All at once the bear stood up and took his head off. It was Avram, the bear trainer. "We do have some trained bears," he said. "But when we have meetings I dress up like a bear and I'm the lookout. That way I can warn the others and give them a chance to get a way while we scare away anybody who might hurt us. Did you really think I was a bear?"

"Of course," Sarah said, and I nodded.

"Once I got a job pretending to be a bear at a fair," said Avram. "I was supposed to fight with this real bear."

"Weren't you scared?" I asked.

"Oi was I scared," said Avram. "I was so scared that as the bear came toward me I began to say the prayer Jews say when they think they will die, Shma Yisroel –"

"What happened?" said Sarah.

"The other bear put his head down by mine. I thought for sure he was going to bite me. But he just whispered in my year."

"What did he say?" I said.

He said, "Shut up - you think you're the only Jew from Smorgon who has to make a living?"

"Did that really happen?" Sarah said.

"Would I lie to you?" said Avram and everybody laughed.

"Now then," said Kate. "Duvidka and Sarachka, what are you doing here? You know you're not permitted to come here. Avram is not the only bear in these woods."

"We only see you on Shabbos," I said.

"We just wanted to be with you," Sarah said.

"We come here for our Bund meetings," said Anna. "It's not safe for us to meet in our houses, but this is not a place for children. We bring Dvoira because she's old enough to understand and help with what we do. She'll take you home now. But you both must promise two things. You must promise never to tell anybody how to get here. And you must forget whom you saw here today with us. You must promise because if you tell anyone it would be dangerous for us and dangerous for you."

We promised we wouldn't tell.

"And if you don't tell Papa and Mama where you were today," said Kate, "we won't tell them either."

Dvoira took us home through the woods. It was Spring, the days were getting very long, and all through the woods were blue and yellow and red wild flowers and tiny strawberries were spreading all over the ground. She had a basket with her and on the way home we gathered the little strawberries. That way if anyone saw us, they would think we just came into the woods to pick berries.

When we got close to Karka we circled around so it would look like we were coming from the direction of Smorgon. We didn't have to worry much about being seen. Most of the men had gone back to the synagogue in Smorgon for afternoon services and would not be back until sundown and Mama was visiting a neighbor's house with some of the ladies.

When Mama came home, we were playing with some friends. "Did you children have a nice afternoon?" she said. "I hope you didn't get into any mischief."

"Oh no, Mama," we both said. "We wouldn't do that. We helped Dvoira pick some strawberries."

Mama washed the berries and gave us each a bowl of berries to eat with sour cream. "I can sell the rest of the berries in the market tomorrow," said Mama.

When our older sisters came home, they acted like they hadn't seen us since morning and helped Mama get ready for our evening meal. Pretty soon Papa came home and some of the other men came into our house. Mama said the blessings over the bread and the wine. Papa lit the Havdalah candle, the twisted candle that is lit at the end of Shabbos. Because we couldn't do any work on Shabbos, the meal was a cold one: boiled potatoes, bread, some boiled eggs, herring and pickles.

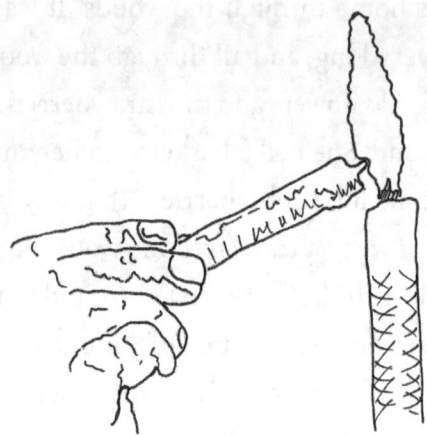

After dinner Maish taught us some new Yiddish songs he'd learned. He was careful not to sing any that would upset Papa. It was such a wonderful evening that I started to complain when Mama told me to get ready for bed, but Dvoira winked at me and I decided not to make a fuss.

That night I dreamed about bears in the woods but instead of being frightened I became Avram in my dream and talked Yiddish to the bears and taught them to pull wagons and stand on their front feet and dance around. And I remember wondering if there were bears in America.

Four

Chanukah: December 1903

Next to Simchas Torah I like Chanukah best. Papa says it's not an important Jewish holiday and it's only because it comes around the time of Christmas that we make much fuss about it. Of course Kate and Anna have a different view. They say Chanukah is the story of Jews who fought the armies of King Antiochus. He was like the Russian Czar of those times. He wanted the Jews to dress and act like Greeks and bow down to the Greek Gods. Judah Maccabee and his brothers got all the Jews together to drive out the Greek soldiers. Kate says the Jews of Smorgon can fight the bosses of the factories and soldiers of the Czar.

Chanukah comes at the beginning of winter when the days get very short and the nights get very long in Smorgon. Around Chanukah, when we get up it's dark and the sun is only up a few hours before it starts to get dark again.

Chanukah lasts for eight nights. We have a candle holder, a menorah, with places for eight candles and one more to hold the candle we light the others with. Every night we light one more candle in the menorah. One the first night, two the second night, until on the last night we light eight candles.

Papa says that we light candles to celebrate a miracle that happened long ago. When the Jews drove the Greek soldiers out of Judea, they found the Greek soldiers had made a mess of the temple in Jerusalem. When they cleaned it up, they needed to light the lamps in the temple but they could only find enough olive oil to last for one night. But a miracle happened. The oil lasted for eight nights until they could get more olive oil.

In Smorgon, Christian children get presents from somebody called Father Christmas. We get Chanukah gelt - money. Sarale and I would each get a kopek from Papa on the first night of Chanukah. Sometimes, if there were guests, they would also give us each a kopek.

On this particular Chanukah, when I was six and a half, I got an idea. I would get enough Chanukah gelt to buy myself a special toy I saw in the market. It was a hoop with a stick. You use the stick to make the hoop roll.

I said to Papa, "You need to give me two kopeks the second night and four the third night and eight the next night. Each night you should give me twice as many as the night before."

"And how many kopeks would you have all together at the end?" said Papa.

"A lot," I said. "Enough to buy a toy I saw in the market."

"Can you figure out exactly how many kopeks you would have?" said Maish "If you got one the first night and two the second night what would you have?"

"Three," I said.

And four more the next night? "Seven," I said.

"So," said Maish. "Double each night. How many will you have on the eighth night?"

I thought for a long time. And then I said, "255 kopeks."

"That's right," said Maish. Everybody clapped for me.

"Very good, my clever boy," said Mama. "There's only one problem with your idea. We don't have 255 kopeks. You're lucky to get one kopek."

Everybody laughed but I didn't think it was funny. Papa has a saying. "It's not a shame to be poor, but it's not an honor either." In America I would become rich but it wouldn't hurt to start before I got there.

Most nights of the year we had potatoes for dinner. Mama took the skins off and boiled them. Some night that's all we had, with, maybe, a piece of black bread and a little butter. One of Maish's friends wrote a song about potatoes too. In Yiddish potatoes are bulbas. Here's the potato song:

> *Sunday bulbas*
> *Monday bulbas*
> *Tuesday and Wednesday bulbas*
> *Over and over, bulbas*
> *Shabbos for a real treat,*

A bulba kugela
Sunday once again bulbas

A kugela is a little kugel and a kugel is a pudding. You can make them from noodles or matzah but I liked potato kugels the best. Mama's kugels are crispy and brown on the outside and soft in the middle. During the eight days of Chanukah, Mama makes delicious pancakes from potatoes. We call the pancakes latkes. For potato pancakes you peel the raw potatoes and then rub them over something Mama calls her "ribeisen." It's a piece of metal with lots of little raised edges to cut the potatoes into fine pieces to make the pancake batter. I got to help rubbing the potatoes. You have to be careful how you hold the potatoes or you can scrape some skin off your fingers too.

Mama adds eggs, chopped up onion and salt and pepper to the potatoes. Then she drops spoonfuls into hot fat in her heavy iron frying pan. She knows how to make them so that they're crispy and golden brown all over. We eat them with sour cream or fresh apple sauce that Mama makes from apples our neighbors grow.

Every evening during Chanukah is like a small party. At sundown we'd light the right number of candles and Papa would say a Chanukah prayer. Then we'd sing a Chanukah song and have our potato latkes. And then Sarah and I and some of our friends would play a game of dreidle. You can play dreidle for money. But Mama only lets us play for nuts. First everybody puts a nut in the middle. Then you spin the dreidle. When it stops the Hebrew letter that shows on the top of the dreidle tells you to put two in, take two out, take half, or take all. Sarah and I play and sometimes our other sisters play too. Sometimes, even Mama and Papa play with us.

Chanukah is not a holiday where people get to stay home from work so Kate and Anna only got to be home on Friday night. So on Friday night we had a really big party. Maish came and brought a beef brisket, a wonderful kind of meat that Mama cooked to go with our potato latkes. Some of my sisters' friends came over after dinner and a few gave Sarah and me Chanukah gelt. After we had dinner and lit the Menorah, Maish taught us a new Chanukah song.

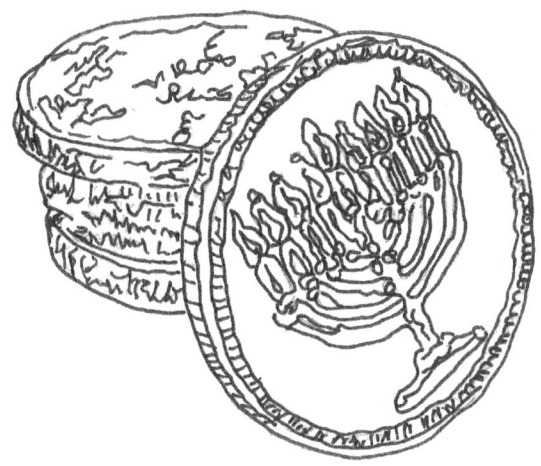

While we were playing dreidle, I kept wishing we were playing for kopeks instead of nuts. All the Jewish kids got a few kopeks for Chanukah gelt. If we played dreidle for money, I could win all their kopeks. Of course, I could also lose. Anyway Mama wouldn't let us play for money.

But then I got a really great idea. I thought of a way to get the other kids' money without playing dreidle. Every Thursday afternoon all of our neighbors started getting ready for Shabbos which starts on Friday night. It was the job of one kid in each family to bring a live chicken to my Papa to kill for their Friday night dinner. There's a special way to kill a chicken for it to be kosher and only somebody like Papa was allowed to do that.

None of the kids liked carrying a live chicken upside down with its feet tied together. The chickens squawked and tried to peck them. And they didn't like watching Papa kill the chickens.

Sometimes they would bring the chickens to me and I would take them to Papa to kill and then I would bring the chicken back to them to take home. Sometimes they'd give me a cookie or a pretty rock for this. But this Chanukah they all had Chanukah gelt. So I decided that each kid would have to pay a kopek for my help with the chickens.

It worked fine. At first the kids didn't want to pay me their Chanukah gelt so I just said, "So carry your own chicken to my Papa." So then they paid me a kopek for each chicken.

Papa was a little surprised when almost every chicken he killed that afternoon was brought to him by me. "How are you so lucky to get this job?" he asked. "I'm just helping my friends," I said.

"The other kids don't like to watch you kill the chickens."

"You're a good boy, my yingele. You'll have lots of friends if you help them when they need your help." I didn't tell Papa I made them pay me. What's the difference if they pay me or not? I'm still helping them.

Finally, one Thursday, which was market day in Smorgon, I had enough to buy the hoop. With my own Chanukah gelt and the money I got from the other kids for the chickens, I had 25 kopeks. Not very many of my friends had any toys they bought. What they had were homemade. They'd all be surprised when they saw me rolling the hoop as I ran by them.

When Mama took me with her that morning I asked her if I could go to Yussele's house to play. But when I got there I told Yussele we were going to the market. I told him I had enough money to buy a hoop and we could play with it after I bought it.

The market was not far from Yussele's house in Smorgon. We found Mrs. Levinsky, the lady who sold toys and I was about to give her my money, when I felt Dvoira's hand on my shoulder. "Mama," she said. "Look who is here." And there were Mama and Sarale too. They were shopping for our Shabbos dinner.

I tried to put the money back in my pocket but Mama caught my hand. "Duvidel, where did you get so much money?"

"It's his Chanukah gelt," said Yussele. "I got three kopeks."

"There's a lot more than that here," said Mama. "Duvidel, tell me the truth. How did you get so much money?"

"I wanted to get this hoop," I said. "So I made each kid pay me a kopek to bring the chickens to Papa. They didn't mind paying me."

Dvoira took my money and counted it. "There's 25 kopeks here," she said. "That's as much as the girls who work in the bagel bakeries make in a whole day. And they have to work 15 hours for that."

Mama turned to Mrs. Levinsky. "Nu, Malka, how much is this toy, It doesn't look like it's very well made. It probably isn't even new."

Mrs. Levinsky looked Mama in the eye. "That hoop comes from the best factory in Minsk," she said. "I go to the fair in Minsk and bring back only the best made toys. I usually sell it for 40 kopeks, but for your clever little boy, who earned his own money, I'll only charge 25 kopeks."

"Never mind," said Mama. "He doesn't have to buy your hoop. We'll go to Mrs. Shapiro who has better toys and better prices. Sell it to some foolish person that doesn't know any better."

I would have been worried because I really wanted that hoop. But I knew what Mama was doing. It's called bargaining. So when Mama started to walk away, Dvoira and Sarale and I went too.

"All right, take it for 20," Mrs. Levinsky said. "I'm losing money but you're a good friend."

"It's not worth more than five," said Mama. "Come, Duvid Mendel." And she kept walking away.

After another ten minutes of going back and forth: 18-6, 17-7 I finally got the hoop for 10 kopeks. I paid Mrs. Levinsky and counted 15 kopeks I had left. I was so happy I had my hoop and I could buy a lot more stuff.

"I saw a knife that I can keep in my pocket," I said, and I started to run toward the knife stall. But Mama's hand caught my collar and pulled me back.

"Hold out your hand with the money," she said. I did what she said and she took 10 kopeks from me. "This is what you give your family to help us give you food and a warm place to sleep."

"Kate and Anna give Mama all of their pay and she gives them back what they need to spend each week," said Dvoira. "I do that too when I do work for our neighbors."

I knew this was only right and I still had five kopeks. "I'm going to buy some candy," I said.

"For one kopek you can buy enough candy to share with Yussele and your sisters," Mama said.

"But if I spend five kopeks I'll get a lot more," I said.

"No," said Mama. "The candy will be gone in no time and you'll have nothing to show for your money. You must think of something that's more sensible."

What could I buy with my four kopeks? Yussele thought I should buy another toy but Mama said one was enough. Then Dvoira said, "Follow me. I know just the thing for my clever little brother."

She led us to the bookseller. "But can I get a book for 4 kopeks?" I said.

"Only an old torn one," said Dvoira. "But you can buy a copy book to write in. You can keep track of all the money you make with your ideas and you can practice your writing. I'll help you."

So that's how I got the copy book that I'm writing in now to remember what happened to me and my family in Karka and Smorgon.

Mama finished her shopping and I was proud that she had my 10 kopeks to buy extra things for our Shabbos dinner. Then we took Yussele home and he and I took turns rolling the hoop so his family could see my new toy.

When we got to our house, Papa heard the story of the money I made and the hoop and copy book I bought. I could see he wasn't too angry. But he took his time before he talked to me and he spoke in a very serious voice.

"Our neighbors pay me to kill their chickens," he said. "They are generous with us and share what they grow. You must not make their children give you their Chanukah gelt for helping them bring me chickens. We're all poor here and we help each other. Your friends should enjoy their Chanukah gelt. They only get it once a year."

I promised Papa I would not make my friends pay for my help. I also promised I would let them have turns playing with my hoop. And I did. Three turns for one kopek.

Five
Mixing in: The Strike on May Day, 1904

It happened when I was just about seven years old. Sarale and I were helping Mama clean up her milk buckets and get ready for dinner. We asked Mama if we could go pick some of the pretty flowers that were starting to come up along the road. Spring was coming. The days were getting longer. And a misty rain was falling.

We hadn't gotten very far when we saw someone far down the

road coming from Smorgon. Sarale said, "I think I see Kate and Anna coming home."

"It can't be," I said. "They only come home on Friday night and today is only Tuesday."

But it was them. "Hurray!" called Kate when she saw us.

"Hurray for the strike!" Anna shouted. We ran to meet them and they lifted us in the air and twirled us around.

"Down with the Bosses," said Kate.

"No more 15 hours work days," said Anna.

"Hurray for the strike!" they both called out together. And they took my hand and Sara's and we danced around in a circle.

"Hurray for the strike!" we all sang out.

"Hurray for the first of May!" sang Kate and Anna.

Mama came out to see what all the noise was about and they grabbed her hands too and made her dance around in a circle with us.

"Hurray for the First of May!" sang Sarah and me.

"Hurray for May Day!" sang Kate and Anna. "Up with Mama! Down with the Bosses!"

Mama laughed. But she pulled away. "What are you doing home in the middle of the week and what's all the excitement about?"

"We're on strike Mama!"

"You're on strike, Kate?" asked Mama.

"Me too," said Anna.

"You're both on strike?"

"Everybody, Mama. The leather makers. The bagel bakers. All the workshops and factories," said Kate. "We want more pay; we don't want to work so many hours. The leather makers want to be cooler in the summer and warmer in the winter."

"It's May Day, Mama." And they grabbed her and started dancing around in a circle again.

"May Day is when people dance around a pole and put flowers in their hair," said Mama. "What does that have to do with a strike?"

"Not any more. May Day is the day for working people to demand their rights," Anna said. "All over the world working people are marching."

"Even in Vilna?" I said.

"Minsk too?" asked Sarah.

"Even in Moscow, and in St. Petersburg too," Anna replied.

"Really?" I said. "Even in Moscow and St Petersburg? People are marching there too?" I knew those were very big Russian cities far away from Smorgon. "But what is all the marching about?"

"About workers telling their bosses they want to work fewer hours and get more pay," said Anna.

"About safer and cleaner places to work," said Kate.

"That's why we're having a strike. We won't go back to work until the bosses give us what we want."

"But not in America," I said. "In America everybody has good jobs and makes a lot of money."

Kate and Anna laughed. "Why are you laughing?" I said angrily. "Nobody would have a reason to march and strike in America!"

"May Day started in Chicago in America," said Anna. "They had a strike just like we're having. They want more pay and less hours to work and they want children in schools instead of working in factories and mines."

I never heard of "Chicago" until that first day of May in 1904. Chicago is a hard name to pronounce in Yiddish or in Russian. It's spelled a funny way in English too. The sound at the beginning sounds like the beginning of shlemazl in Yiddish someone who always has bad luck.

"So if children work in factories and mines and working people have strikes," I said, "why do people want to go to America?"

"In America," said Kate, "everybody has the same rights as everybody else. But they still have to get money for food and a place to live. So they have to work. And sometimes their bosses make them work too hard."

Just then Papa came home from the synagogue in Smorgon where he had been studying. He already knew about the strike and he didn't look happy. "You want higher pay? Strike! You don't like your boss? Strike! You want two Saturdays in every week? Strike!"

"Papa," said Anna, "we just want to be treated like somebody, like a mensch. It's our right."

As usual, Mama saw an argument coming and cut it off. "Come, I have to put some more water in the soup. We've got unexpected guests for dinner. Sarale, come and help. Duvidel, run down to Mrs. Shulman's and ask if she could spare a few potatoes and on the way back get a loaf of bread from the baker. Tell him I'll pay Friday."

After dinner some friends of Kate and Anna's came to our house. Maish came and Avram and a friend of my sister Anna named Dunya. Maish sang a new song in Yiddish about May Day and then Dunya sang a Russian Song about the birch trees that grew in the woods of Smorgon. Then they talked about the May Day meeting that was planned for the next day in Smorgon. All the strikers would be there, and an important woman was coming from Vilna to speak. They called her Chavera Froidela. And a man named Comrade Vladamir was coming from Minsk. But what was most exciting was that Anna had been chosen to speak for the workers in the bagel bakeries.

When Papa heard that, he was very angry. "I forbid it!" he said. "Do you want to get yourself killed? Besides, what have you got to say at such a meeting? You're only a young girl."

"The girls who work in the bagel bakeries elected her," said Kate. "They like the way she talks up for them. They like her courage."

"Courage?" said Papa. "You mean foolishness. Anna, Kate, you may not go to this meeting. None of us will go. I'm the Papa and I say no speech and no meeting for us."

Maish tried to calm Papa down. "It's only a public meeting, Reb Yankle Laib, a rally to support the strike. Even your neighbors, the farmers of Karka will come. You are their Rabbi. You should be with them. Anna is a very good speaker. We're all proud of her. And there will be young men to protect her and make sure there is no trouble at the rally."

"Jews shouldn't mix in the troubles of the gentiles," said Papa.

"They're our troubles too, Papa. Our motto is 'Workers of the World Unite!' If we stick together, the bosses have to listen!" Anna shouted.

"We'll all be there," said Dunya. "The Jewish workers, the Christians, the Gypsies - all the working people, farmers - everyone. All of us together can make a better world."

Papa started to shout now - "I forbid–"

But before he could continue Mama put her hand on his arm. "It's only a May Day celebration," she said. "We'll make a basket of food to take with us to celebrate the holiday. We'll join with our neighbors. So there will be a few speeches. So Anna will speak for the bagel bakery women. Admit it, Yankle Laib, you're proud that she's been chosen. Who should they choose if not our Anna? In the bible there are stories of many brave Jewish women who spoke out for their people. We'll go, all but Sarah and Duvid who are too young for such things."

"But, Mama!" Sarah and I called out together. "We want to go to the rally. We want to hear Anna," said Sara.

"It's not fair!" I said.

Papa gave us his special evil-eye look. "All right, we'll go together except for Sarah and Duvid. But if there's any sign of trouble we'll all come home."

Sarah gave a quick look at me that said don't argue.

Anna threw her arms around Mama and tried to kiss Papa but he pushed her away. "Get away! Such a girl," he said, but he couldn't help a little smile.

After that there was more singing and even Papa joined in. Sarah nodded to me and we slipped out of the room.

"It's not fair!" I said to her again.

"Sha, quiet," she said. "When everybody is gone, you and I will go too. There will be so many people there we can make sure Papa and Mama don't see us. We'll hide behind the speakers' platform and leave before everybody else so we can be home before the rest of the family."

I gave Sarah a hug.

"That's a great plan. We'll hear Anna and the others and we'll have an adventure and no one will know!" I said.

"Sha," said Sarah.

The next morning Sarah and I did our chores and acted really unhappy that we weren't going to the May Day rally. Mama packed a food basket. And our neighbors began to gather outside our house. Each different group of workers was marching together to the square in the middle of Smorgon and the farmers had come to ask Papa to lead their group.

"Did you know that your Anna is going to speak for the bagel bakers?" said Reb Shimon, one of the farmers.

"Of course," said Papa. "She asked my permission and I gave it. Who better than Anna to speak?"

Sarah and I could hardly keep from showing our excitement. But we waited until the farmers had marched off followed by the rest of the families in Karka. Then we took the food Mama had left for us, wrapped it in Sarah's babushka, her head scarf, and went toward Smorgon. But we circled around on a little side path away from the main road. When we got to Smorgon, we found a place between some houses a little way from the square where we could see each group of workers marching into the square but not be seen by the rest of our family.

It was like the best holiday ever. Each group had banners and signs. The klezmer were playing happy music. Some of the marchers were singing songs. People going through the crowd were selling food and May Day flowers. We saw Avram with a trained bear pulling a cart in the parade and leading the bear trainers but he didn't see us. And there was Anna leading the women and girls from the bagel bakeries. She carried a red flag that said, "Bagel bakery workers" on it in Yiddish and Russian. Behind her was Dunya with a sign in Russian. I figured out it said, "Striking for the 12 hour day," and another sign said, "Defend the rights of the working people."

By the time everybody reached the square we had never seen so many people in one place. They weren't all from Smorgon. There were people from every little village in the whole area. There was a light drizzle falling but nobody seemed to care.

Sarah and I moved carefully around the crowd making sure nobody saw us from the family until we were behind the platform that had been built for the speakers. While we waited for the speeches to start, we ate the food we brought with us.

Then we heard klezmer musicians on the stage and a group of people began to sing the Bund Anthem. Maish's voice stood out clearly above the others. Then another group sang a Russian song, "The Warshavyarka."

"To the bloody battle, sacred and just, march forward working people!"

After that, came the speakers. Chavera Froidela spoke in Yiddish and Russian. Comrade Vladimir spoke in Belarussian. Other speakers from each of the worker's groups spoke in whatever language they chose. After every speaker, there were loud cheers. We could see young men with red armbands around the platform and the edges of the crowd. I expected to see some policemen or soldiers but there weren't any. Smorgon only had a few policemen and Maish had told me that some of them secretly supported the strike.

Then it was Anna's turn. Like the others she talked about the long hours and bad conditions of the workers. She told about how the women and girls in the bagel bakery had to work 14-15 hours a day, six days a week for 50 kopeks a day. She told about how women in Smorgon had started the Movement for a 12 hour day, how girls much younger than herself worked the same long hours for 25 kopeks. She told about two girls who got tuberculosis because the air was bad in the bakeries. She and the other bagel bakers had trouble with their eyes because very little light came into bakeries and there was no electricity. Then she read a poem she had written herself.

We bagel bakers earn little pay
We work through the night and half the day,
We grind and knead and boil and bake
And produce the profits the bosses take

The kettles are hot, the ovens too
And always there seems to be too much to do
Our bagels are sold throughout the lands
But little of the money stays in our hands

So now women and girls have taken the lead
to strike against the bosses greed
We want shorter hours and better pay
And until we get them, on strike we'll stay.

When she finished, the whole square was silent for a minute and then people cheered and began to chant: "Strike! Strike! Strike!" The echoes of the chant bounced off the two story brick buildings that surrounded the square where most of the owners of the bakeries and the factories lived.

Then the leader of the leather workers got up to speak and Sarah and I decided it was time for us to head home.

We moved away from the square toward the next street so we could go around the crowd and not be seen. And then we heard the sound of horses and men's voices. We quickly ran between two houses and peeked out at the street. There were more police than we'd ever seen. They must have been sent in from Vilna or Minsk. The Smorgon police were there too. The police were in rows with clubs in their hands. And in front of them all were a group of Cossacks on horses.

Sarah whispered to me, "Can you hear what they're saying?"

"Sha!" I said, and we both strained to hear the voices. A man on a horse was talking and the others became quiet. He was speaking Russian and saying something about teaching the strikers a lesson. We somehow knew he was telling them that when he gave a signal they were to charge the crowd in the square.

"We've got to warn them," said Sarah.

"But what about Papa?" I said. "We're not supposed to be here."

"We can't worry about that now," said Sarah. And we began running toward the square.

When we got near the speaker's platform we began shouting as loud as we could, "The Cossacks are coming! The police are coming!"

Avram appeared in front of us with his cart and bear.

"I can hold them off for a few minutes," he said. "Warn your sister and the other speakers. They're the ones they're after."

Some of the young men with the red armbands formed a line behind Avram and his bear facing where the police would be coming from. We ran to the front of the platform and ran right into Maish and Dunya. "100's of police are coming! And Cossacks on horses!" I shouted.

"Stay with me," said Dunya. Maish called to the men with red arm bands on the platform and they quickly got all the speakers off the stage and Dunya began to run toward the side of the square where the Orthodox Church stood. People scattered to make room for Dunya and us and the speakers who were following. And then they quickly moved together behind us. When she reached the church Dunya headed around the side to a door that led down to the basement. We all followed.

"Oh it's locked!" screamed Sarah. But Dunya took a key from her pocket and unlocked the door. We all followed Dunya into the basement of the church. She gave Maish the key and told him to go out and lock the door from the outside. Then Maish went to the front of the church and acted like he had just come out of the front door to see what was happening. Inside Dunya went toward the back of the church until she came to what looked like a solid wall. On the wall was a ring and when she turned it a door opened and we went through it. We were in a room with benches around the wall and a small lamp in one corner so we could barely see.

With the door safely closed, Kate and Anna came up to Sarah and me. "You disobeyed Papa," said Anna.

"We wanted to hear you speak. You were wonderful!" Sarah said.

"You two could have been hurt yourselves," said Kate.

"But we knew we had to warn you when we saw the police," I said.

Just then I felt a big hand on my shoulder. It was the man they called Comrade Vladimir. His other hand was on Sarah's shoulder.

"So who are these young heroes who gave us the warning? Do you use children in Smorgon as lookouts?" he said.

"This is Duvid and Sarah, my brother and sister," said Anna. "They weren't supposed to come to the rally and they were trying to get home without Papa seeing them. Fortunately for all of us they took the long way home."

Outside the church we could hear running feet, horses, curses, and people crying out in pain. Then we heard noisy feet walking above us and loud voices. The police were searching for the speakers. They sounded very angry that the speakers had gotten away so quickly. We all held our breath and didn't make a sound. Then we heard the priest's voice. He sounded calm but angry. I couldn't tell what he was saying. After a while the noise above stopped and we could hear the police leaving the church.

It seemed like hours before the door to our room opened. It was the priest, Father Vasily.

"Do you think it's safe for us to come out now, Papa?" said Dunya.

Father Vasily said, "The police are on their way back to Vilna."

"You call your priest 'Papa'?" I said.

Dunya laughed. "He is my Papa. How do you think I had the key to the basement door?"

Chavera Froidela thanked Father Vasily for hiding them. "I didn't hide you," he said. "My daughter did. What can a father do with such a child? She thinks that a church should be concerned about the suffering of working people."

Dunya said to her father, "These are the children of Rabbi Yankle Laib Gutman."

"I know your father," he said. "A scholar and a good man. We talk often about our disobedient children."

Anna and Kate took us home. Dvoira met us outside our house. They'd been waiting for us. "You're all OK?" asked Dvoira.

"Yes, our plan worked thanks to the warning these two were able to give us," said Anna. "Dunya hid us and her father ordered the police to leave his church."

"Papa is more worried than angry," said Dvoira. "We saw you two come running and yelling that the police were coming. We were all watching the rally from the steps of the synagogue and went inside when the trouble started. The police came in and went through everything but Papa and the other rabbis said there was nothing for them to find and they finally left. I explained Dunya's plan for hiding the speakers if there was trouble."

"Wasn't Anna wonderful? Didn't you love her poem?" I said when I saw Papa.

"Wonderful, wonderful," he muttered. "And what are your mother and I to do with two children who don't stay where they are told to stay? What would have happened to you and to all of us if the police had caught you?"

"It's my fault," said Sarah. "I got Duvidel to go with me. It was my idea to go hear Anna."

I was about to object. I didn't like the idea of Sarah taking credit for the whole thing. But I decided it was best to keep my mouth shut.

Kate got the last word. "I know, Papa, you don't agree with the strike and what your daughters do but I also know you are a courageous man yourself in fighting for what you believe and you take pride in us."

Actually Mama got the last word. "One slice of black bread for your supper and to bed, both of you. And in the morning we'll talk about the extra chores you'll have for the next month."

As we were finishing our bread, we heard running footsteps and a knock on our door.

"Who's there?" Anna called out. "It's me, Dunya, Let me in."

"The police have arrested Maish," she said when Anna opened the door. "He's in jail now with some of the rally leaders."

So that was our first May Day. In our place, on the stove, I whispered to Sarah, "It wasn't all your idea."

"It really was my idea. Anyway we're heroes," she said. "Do you think we'll get medals?"

"I'd settle for a bowl of Mama's chicken soup," I said.

I didn't sleep well that night and I had a dream that Sarah and I were riding Cossack horses and chasing the Cossacks out of Smorgon and everyone was cheering for us. But then the Czar suddenly appeared on a huge black horse. The funny thing was he looked like Papa.

"I'll teach you to disobey your Papa!" he shouted. Then he took a rope like an American cowboy and threw it around Sarah and me and dragged us off our horses.

"Duvid Mendel, wake up! Wake up!" Sarah was shaking me. "Stop kicking me."

I opened my eyes and for a minute I didn't know where I was.

"You were rolling around and kicking me and mumbling something about the Czar. That must have been some nightmare."

Six
The Wedding: May 3, 1904

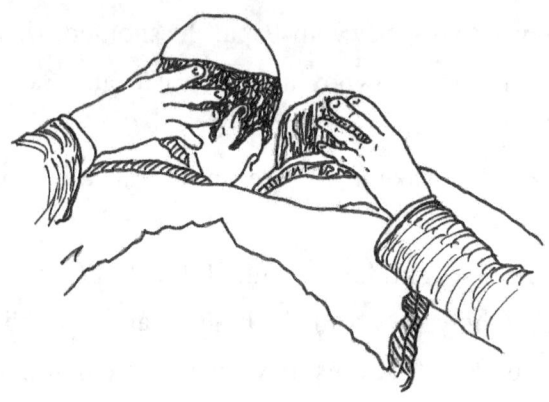

The day after the May Day rally, there were only police on the streets of Smorgon. For our family there was good news and bad news.

The bad news was that the Czar's police arrested some of the leaders and took them to prison in Minsk. They were getting ready to send them to Siberia. Maish was arrested too.

The good news was that Maish was in jail in Smorgon.

More bad news: they arrested Kate and kept her in jail overnight. They wanted her to tell what she knew about Maish and the others.

More good news: Papa went down to the jail with the other

rabbis and brought Kate home.

The bad news was the police were looking for Anna.

The good news was that Dunya was keeping her hidden.

More bad news: When she got home Kate said she had something important to tell us. "Maish has to leave Smorgon and I'm going with him."

"They're sending him to Siberia? You can't go with him to Siberia! I forbid it!" shouted Papa.

"No, Papa," said Kate. "They want to send Maish to Siberia but his father gave some money to the chief of the Smorgon police. He's going to let him escape. We have to leave right away."

"But where will you go?" said Mama. "How will we know where you are?"

"We're going to America," said Kate. "Maish has an uncle in Chicago. Maish's Papa will pay for us to go. Our friends will help us get across the border to Germany. When we get to America, I'll write to you."

"But Maish's father is a boss," I said. "He has a leather factory. Why would he give you money?"

"He's a Papa too," said Kate. "He knows we have to leave Smorgon. He wants us to be safe."

"But why do you have to go?" said Mama.

"If I stay, I'll be arrested again soon myself. There is a revolution coming. Besides we love each other."

"It's not right for a young man and a young woman to travel together who aren't married," said Papa.

"We want to be married," said Kate. "But we can't now, Papa. It's the 49 days of the Omer. We'll have to find a rabbi to marry us in Chicago."

Now I have to explain. In Smorgon we have two calendars. We have the Jewish calendar and we have the calendar that the government and the Christians use. May Day was the first of May on that calendar in 1904. But it was the 16th day of Iyyar on the Jewish calendar in the year 5664. In the Jewish calendar we have seven weeks, 49 days, that are sad days. We're supposed to remember a lot of bad things that happened to Jews. Bad things happened to Jews in every part of the year but during these 49 days really bad things happened. We start counting the 49 days on the second day of Passover. It's called the 49 days of Omer. There can't be any celebrations during the whole 49 days. And that means no weddings. But there is one day in the Omer called Lag B'omer - the 33rd day when there can be happy times. When I was three years old, I got my first haircut on Lag B'omer.

"Papa," I said. "Good news! They can get married tomorrow! It's Lag B'omer."

Kate hugged me, "Oh, you're a clever boy, of course it's Lag B'omer. Papa you can marry us tomorrow."

Sarah was excited, "Papa, don't you see. It's fate. Maish and Kate were meant to be married."

"We can't have a wedding tomorrow," said Mama. "We have no dowry for you. Maish's father will expect us to give Maish money to marry you."

"Times are changing Mama," said Kate. "We don't need a dowry. Maish knows I love him and he loves me. That's enough."

"Of course," said Papa. "Everything is changing. You don't need money to live. You can live on love. And when will your beloved ask for my permission to marry you?"

"He would ask your permission but the police have him in jail.

Papa, we want you to marry us tomorrow," said Kate.

"Tomorrow is too soon," said Mama. "There isn't time to make food, find you a wedding dress, invite the guests."

"We don't have time. And it can't be an ordinary wedding," said Kate. "If the police hear about it, they'll arrest Maish again. Papa and Mama, please understand. We want to be married before we leave but we must leave before the police know what is happening."

Papa closed his eyes and seemed to be thinking. We all got very quiet and looked at Papa. We all knew we couldn't interrupt Papa when he was thinking.

Finally Dvoira said, "Papa?" very quietly.

He waved his arm but kept his eyes closed.

When he opened them, he said, "Tomorrow, as we do every year, all of Karka will go into the woods for Lag B'omer. We will sing, we will dance, the children will play games, we will share some food, drink some kvass and some wine."

"But Papa," said Kate, "the wedding."

"We will all go into the woods," said Papa, "and if the police should see us go, they'll say 'There go those Jews into the woods with their strange ways and strange holidays.'"

We all laughed.

"This is all happening too fast," Mama said with tears in her eyes. "I've thought for years about my daughters' weddings and now look at what is happening. When will you leave us?"

"Tonight, as soon as it's dark, Maish will escape," Kate said. "The chief will leave his cell door unlocked and the other police will be eating their supper. Avram and Dunya have found a safe place for him to stay for tonight. I'll get word to Maish's family to join us in the woods so they can see us get married. Anna will meet us there too. We'll have to leave right after the wedding ceremony. We can't take the train from here. Avram will take us on horses to Vilna and our friends in the movement will get us to Germany where we can get a ship."

"You have it all worked out," said Papa. "You expect your mother and me to just say 'Mazel Tov' and let you get married in such a way and run off to America. I told you over and over you shouldn't mix in. You say 'times are changing Papa.' You say 'It isn't our fault, Papa. The Czar is making us do this. The bosses are making us do this.'"

Sarah and I ran to Kate and hugged her. Mama started to cry and pretty soon everybody was crying. Even Papa's eyes looked wet.

Papa sat down with his hands raised to the roof. "God in heaven!" he said. "What have I done that you punish me like this? My whole world is upside down. My daughters have chosen lives I don't understand. They don't even ask my permission to do what they do. This one gets in trouble with the police. That one tells me she will be married. Even my little ones disobey me. Now my family will be torn apart. And they do not even ask my blessing."

I had never seen Papa like this. He seemed so sad.

"They have to go, Papa, and they want you to marry them," Mama said. "They want your blessing. You can't deny them your blessing. Maish is a good young man. A mensch. They'll take good care of each other."

"A mensch you say?" Papa sounded so angry. "Some mensch who gets arrested and has to run away. Some mensch who asks the woman he loves to marry him like a beggar and run away from her home and her family. I'll marry them. I can't let them go without being married. But my blessing? I'll have to think about that."

"Is Anna going too?" I asked.

"Anna!" cried Mama. "Will she go to America too? I forgot about Anna."

"No, Mama," said Kate. "We begged Anna to go with us. But she says she has to stay. She says she has to be here to lead the bagel bakers and help to bring a revolution. Dunya is keeping her safe. The Czar's police will leave soon and she'll go back to work."

"I have to stay." It was Anna. She was outside the window. She opened the door and came in. Anna hugged Mama and Kate and Sarah and me. But when she went to Papa he pushed her away.

"Get away. You've been too busy with your strike and your revolution to come home to your Mama and Papa."

"Papa." Anna was beginning to cry. "I've been hiding. I didn't want to bring trouble to my family. Tell me you understand and give Kate and me your blessing."

Kate and Anna knelt down on the floor next to Papa. "We want your blessing, we need your blessing," said Anna. "Do you think we want to make you and Mama unhappy? Do you think we want to be away from you?"

"Please give us your blessing," said Kate. "Tell us that you understand why we have to do what we are doing. Give us your blessing."

Papa looked up. "Do I understand? No. Too much is changing too fast. Now you want my blessing? After everything is decided, you want my blessing?"

"Papa, give them your blessing," said Dvoira.

Sarah and I looked at Papa. "Please, Papa," we said.

Mama dried her eyes on her apron. "All this comes so fast. It's hard for your Papa. It's hard for me. Nu, so it's hard for you too. Karka has been our only home. How can I think of Anna in constant danger? How can I think of Kate so far away? How can

I imagine your life? Where will you live? What will you do there? But I want you to be safe and you're not safe here. So go and take my broken heart with you. I wish Anna were going too. But know that your Papa blesses you even if he doesn't say so."

"Did I say I wouldn't give my blessing? I said I'd think about it. So I thought about it," Papa said.

Papa put a hand on Anna's head and on Kate's. And then he said in Hebrew. "Lord our God, king of the universe, bless these, my daughters. Keep Anna safe in what she does. Keep Kate safe on her long journey. Bless the young man who takes my daughter from me. Bring them all safely to their new home. And we pray that you will one day soon bring us all together in peace, Amen."

"Amen," we all said. And then there was a lot of hugging and kissing and crying.

Papa sent Sarah and me to remind all our neighbors that the next day was Lag B'omer and we would all be going to the woods. "Remember, it's for Lag B'omer," he said. "Don't say anything about a wedding."

He didn't need to tell us. We knew what to say and what not to say. But our little farm community is a funny place.

"Just a moment," Mrs. Ginsberg said, when I told her about Lag B'omer. "Here are a few eggs for your Mama and Papa."

At the next house Mrs. Rozinsky had some potatoes for me to take home. From Reb Chaim I got a live chicken which I carried upside down by its tied legs. By the time we got home, Sarah and I were so loaded with good things we could hardly walk.

Mama didn't seem surprised. Our neighbors often gave us small gifts. That's the way they paid Papa for his services as Rabbi and teacher. But this day they seemed more generous than I could remember. What did they know and how did they know it?

That night we had one of Mama's wonderful meals. Chicken soup with kreplach - noodle dough filled with kasha and boiled in the soup, chicken, a carrot tzimis, potatoes roasted with the chicken, the first small cucumbers from a neighbor's garden and a honey cake from one of our neighbors. It was a holiday meal but Mama only made kreplach at sad times. I thought a lot about that. She kept herself busy but inside she must have been feeling very sad.

Dvoira and Sarah listened as Kate and Anna talked about their plans. They asked Kate what she was going to wear for her wedding and worried that they didn't have anything nice enough to wear to a wedding. Kate explained that none of us could wear anything that we wouldn't be wearing to an ordinary outing in the woods. We couldn't run the risk of attracting any attention.

After dinner, Sarah and I were sent to bed but no one else slept that night. Papa prayed a lot and studied his books. Mama made what preparations she could for the wedding and she and Anna helped pack the clothes Kate could carry with her.

The next day was wonderful. Because it was a holiday, the morning service in the shul was almost as full as on Shabbos. The boys that Papa taught came and played around our house even though there were no lessons. The girls were busy helping their Mamas as they usually did but on this day they were packing up food for the celebration in the woods. And in spite of everything Mama was up early delivering her milk.

Anna slipped out early in the morning too and we didn't see her again until we all got to the clearing in the woods where we had our Lag B'omer celebrations every year. When we and the other Karka families got to the clearing she was already there with Dunya and some young men who were scattered around the edges of the clearing. Some of them had been wearing red armbands at the rally but this day they didn't have them on.

Maish's parents, the Krupnicks, and his two brothers and two sisters came a little after we did. They were all wearing nicer clothes than the rest of us. It surprised me that our neighbors, even the kids, didn't pay much attention to their arrival. I guess Papa must have passed the word quietly not to be surprised at anything that might happen.

All the kids played tag and hide and seek with their Mamas warning them not to go too far from the clearing. Then Dvoira and some of the older girls started doing some folk dances. They sang as they danced. Some of the older boys who were studying at the Yeshiva in Smorgon danced some circle dances with their arms on each other's shoulders. Two young men who had been sitting on the edge of the clearing had mandolins and another had a balalika. They began to sing songs in Russian, Belarussian and Yiddish. Dunya sang a Belarussian love song with them. My four sisters sang a Yiddish song about a girl who follows her husband to America.

Suddenly there was a kind of stifled scream from one end of the clearing and people were moving quickly away from that end. And then I saw the reason. Some gypsies and a bear came into the clearing. They brought the bear right into the middle of the clearing and the bear got up and danced while the gypsies formed a circle around the bear and beat out rhythms on their tambourines. I laughed when I realized that Maish and Avram were among the gypsies.

When the bear stopped dancing, Avram tied it to a tree near the opening to the clearing and gave it some apples and bread to eat.

Papa got up then and he said a short Lag B'omer prayer. People spread out blankets and settled down on them in front of Papa.

Papa gave a short talk to everybody there. He talked about a lot in a short time. He talked about fathers and sons: Abraham and Isaac, Jacob and his sons. He talked about Judith and Deborah and other brave women of the Torah. And then he talked about how Moses had led the Jews out of slavery in Egypt. He talked about how Jews had been forced through history to wander from place to place and somehow managed to keep being Jews and following the laws of the Torah and the teachings of the Talmud. And he asked the congregation to join him in a special prayer for those who had left Smorgon for America and the Holy Land and who might be leaving in the future. And he finished with a prayer for peace - that the working people of Smorgon would win their goal to be treated well without suffering and bloodshed.

When Papa finished his prayer for peace, he looked down at our neighbors sitting around the clearing and said, "My friends and neighbors, it would be my honor and that of my family if you would share a moment of great joy and great sadness for us. Because of the time and place in which we live, I ask you to avoid any noise that could suggest to anyone passing by that anything unusual is happening here. Come forward my children."

Kate and Maish got up and stood before him.

Someone was always getting married in Karka or Smorgon so I'd been to quite a few weddings. And I'd seen my father perform weddings before. But this wedding was not like any other I'd seen. First of all they weren't dressed for a wedding. Kate had dressed for a day in the woods and Maish wore his gypsy clothes. Usually there is a Chupah, a canopy, that the couple stands under. At this wedding, four tall young men each held a corner of what looked like a table cloth over the couple. Usually there is a katuba, a wedding contract, written on a scroll. When Maish and Kate came in front of Papa, Maish took a folded paper out of his pocket that he and Kate had prepared in jail and they and Papa signed it on top of a tree stump. Usually, the wedding party walks around the Chupah seven times. Papa stopped them after two and said, "OK, enough." Usually when the rabbi asks the questions and the bride and groom reply "I do," people call out "Mazel Tov," and at the end the groom stamps on a glass and breaks it and everybody cheers.

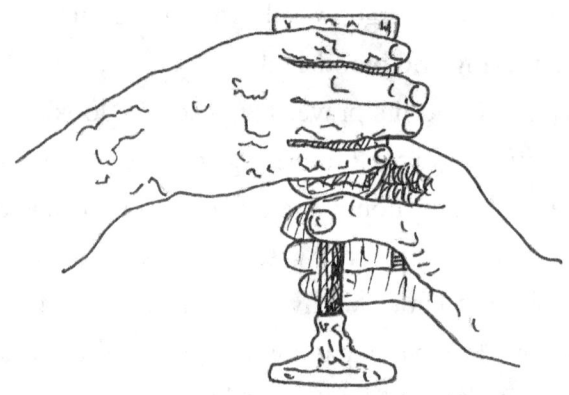

And usually after the wedding ceremony there is singing and dancing and tables of good food. If this had been an ordinary wedding the other rabbis from Smorgon and even relatives from other towns would have come for the wedding. But the wedding was over in just a few minutes. The glass Maish stamped on didn't make much noise because it was laying on soft dirt. Finally, when Papa said, "I now pronounce you husband and wife according to the laws of Moses and Israel," our family and Maish's came up and hugged and kissed them and then everybody very quietly came and said, "Mazel Tov." Then they sat back down on their blankets to eat the food they'd brought for Lag B'omer.

One of the gypsies asked for everyone's attention. I recognized him as Comrade Vladimir even though he was dressed like a gypsy. He congratulated Kate and Maish and their families on the wedding. He said he was speaking not only for himself as their friend but for their comrades in the movement. He said a lot of other things using a lot of big words about strikes and revolutions which I couldn't quite follow. But I remember how he finished.

He said, "I ask you to raise your glasses to drink a toast." Everybody raised their glasses no matter what they were drinking. Like me, a lot of the kids raised imaginary glasses.

"As you say in Yiddish, L' Chaim - to life. As we say in Russian Na Zdarovya - to health. And as we revolutionaries say - to the liberation of the working class."

Then Kate and Maish kissed and everybody clapped as the gypsies formed a circle around them and we all sang, "Hasan, Kallah, Mazel Tov" - "Good luck to the bride and groom."

Maish held his and Kate's hands up in the air and said, "And now I am going to dance with my bride." A lot of people gasped. Men didn't dance with women at Jewish weddings. But the three musicians played a lively song and Maish and Kate danced in the middle of the clearing. Then Avram and Dunya joined them and some of their other friends too. Sarah grabbed me and we danced in and out among the big people.

When the dance was over I went over to Papa. He was talking to Maish's Papa. They didn't look very happy. Maish's father was saying, "I don't understand my son. I worked hard in my life. I did it all for my family. I gave him everything, a nice house, a good education. My factory could be his. I treat my workers well, too. I pay as much as any factory owner. I pay for a doctor if they get sick. I give them days off for the holidays. And how does he pay me back? He tells my workers to strike. He gets himself put in jail. And who has to come to get him out and give him money to run away? His Papa, the evil boss! Your daughter is a nice girl. Maybe now that he's married he'll settle down and be sensible. What do you think, Reb Yankle Laib?"

"What do I think?" Papa replied? "What should I think? My daughter says 'Times change, people change.' And see now in front of me, in front of you, in front of the whole shtetl they danced together. Did they ask your permission to marry? Did they ask mine? Does a son turn against his father? Does a daughter desert her father's ways? Who knows how they'll live their lives in America? Who knows what traif they'll eat, who knows whether they'll get in trouble there too."

"But Papa." I said. And that's all I got to say.

"You," he said. "You, I don't have to listen to. You went to the rally when I told you you couldn't. You see your sisters and you think you can defy me too. You will honor your Papa, you will study and you will live your life as it is written in the Torah and the Talmud." His face scared me. He turned bright red and everybody around heard what he was saying.

Anna came and put her arm around my shoulders. "It's all right, Duvidka. It will be all right."

"But Papa hates me," I said. "He hates us all."

"Papa loves you. He loves us all. But his world is falling apart around him and he doesn't know what to do. We all have to try harder to make him understand," my sister said.

So now I was crying. One thing that was a lot like other weddings was the crying. Usually the mothers cry at weddings. But at my sister Kate's wedding everybody was crying even both Papas. My Papa managed to keep from crying while he was marrying them. But when he was hugging them tears started running down his face. It was so quiet during the ceremony that you could hear people sobbing and Maish's Papa was sighing so loudly my Papa had to give him one of his evil eye looks to quiet him. As people came up to say their quiet Mazel Tovs they were crying.

Everybody in our family was crying. But why should I cry? Kate and Maish were married. Now I finally had a brother. They were going to America where we all would follow and I would become rich. It wasn't until everyone but the families had left and Dunya came to tell Kate and Maish that Avram was waiting in the woods with the horses that I realized that they were really leaving and that I might never see them again that I became really sad and really started sobbing.

For some reason that made everybody laugh. Sarah, who had barely stopped crying herself, said, "Look at the cry baby."

Maish picked me up and swung me around and said, "Don't cry, little brother, you've always been the smart one. You know I'll take good care of your beautiful big sister."

Even Papa put his arm on my shoulder. "Don't cry, yingele," he said. "We've just had a wedding in our family."

"But you're mad at me," I sobbed. Papa looked at me sadly. "I only want you to live a proper life," he said. And then he added, rolling his eyes toward the sky, "God willing."

One last time we hugged Kate and Maish as Dunya warned them they needed to leave. "Baruch ato adonay, Blessed art thou, Oh Lord our God who protects travelers on their journey," Papa said as they went off.

"Go in good health and travel in good health," called Maish's father.

"What will become of them?" said Mama "What will become of us all?"

"What will be, will be," Papa said.

Sarah and I wanted to follow them but Dunya shook her head. "Better to let them go quietly," she said.

In my mind I ran after them and shouted, "See you in America!" It was only in my mind, so they couldn't have heard me. But it made me feel better to imagine they did.

Seven

My First Whole Day Without Food: September 1904

Mama is worried. It's been three months since Kate and Maish left for America and we haven't heard anything from them. Anna found out from a friend in "the movement" that they got on a ship in a place called Hamburg but there have been no letters.

Mama carries her milk every day and keeps cleaning the house even late at night. "Why haven't they written?" she keeps saying. "They must have written to tell us that they got to America. What if their letters get lost? What if they can't find work and they haven't got money? What if …?"

Papa says, "What if we wait to see what God has in store for us? Meanwhile, we have a lot to do for the high holidays. We'll pray to God that they're safe and among friends."

I think he's worried too. But he's the Papa and the rabbi. "What will be, will be," he always says. Another thing he says, particularly to me when I ask his permission to do something, is "If we live, we'll see." Among us Jews, it's considered very dangerous to plan ahead. The evil eye could see and spoil your plans. "Papa," I would say. "Can I go to Smorgon and play with Yussele tomorrow?" I don't know why I even ask. The answer is always the same. "If we live, we'll see."

We don't see Anna much these days. She went back to work in the bagel bakery and sometimes she comes home for dinner on Friday nights. But she often has meetings and she is seldom home on Saturdays at all. There have been more strikes and now I hear Anna and her friends talking about the "Party." When Sarah and I asked Anna if we could come to the party too, she laughed and said, "It's not that kind of a party," and then she looked at us and said very seriously, "You must not say anything to anybody about the party. You could get me and my friends in big trouble."

The nights are colder now in Smorgon, the leaves on the birch trees are turning golden and in the forests there are patches of red, orange, and copper colored bushes and trees. The lake behind our house is too cold to swim in now. But you can see the colors of the leaves in the lake.

I'm still figuring out ways to make some money. The forest just now is full of nuts. I get some of my friends to go with me gathering nuts from the forest. A lot of nuts are just laying on the ground where we just pick them up but for some we have to climb the trees. We have to be careful to watch for the bears because they like the nuts too and Kate told me that bears eat a lot in the fall so they can sleep in their caves all winter. But Avram has taught me how to see where the bears have been by looking for their footprints. I share the nuts with my friends and give some to my mother. But then I sell the rest at the market.

Things aren't good for us in Karka. Our neighbors are poorer than ever. They don't have much to pay Papa. And some families are leaving for America. The strikes keep happening and now people are talking about the revolution. I think Anna's party must have something to do with the revolution. The Czar has a war going on with Japan, I know that's far away but I don't have Maish or Kate here anymore to tell me about it.

I'm worried that the Czar will send Anna to Siberia. Papa still says that the best thing for Jews to do is stick to themselves and stay out of the affairs of the gentiles. I think one reason Anna doesn't come home so much is that she doesn't want to get Papa started again and she doesn't want to worry Mama.

Dvoira, who is about 13 now, also got a job in a bagel bakery. The lady she works for, Malka Rabinowicz says her great-grandmother invented bagels and that the recipe is a family secret. She claims her bagels are the best in Smorgon or any place. Dvoira says all the bagel bakers in Smorgon say their families invented bagels and theirs are the best. In Russian they're called baronoks or baronushkas. That's because they're boiled but we Jews call them bagelach because the baker twists the dough when they're being made. Some people even call them Smorgonkes.

Dvoira works 12 hours, from 2:00 a.m. to 2:00 p.m. because the bagels are made at night to be fresh in the morning. She sleeps in the loft at the bakery with the other bagel bakers and only comes home for Shabbos on Friday afternoon. But she has to be back by 2:00 a.m. Sunday morning.

Papa isn't happy about Dvoira working outside our house. One Friday night Dvoira went to a meeting with Anna and didn't come home until very late. Papa was very angry and at first told her she had to stop working. But our family needs the money she makes so he said she could work if she promised not to go to any more meetings.

Sometimes Sarah and I go to the bagel factory to see the bagels being made. Besides Malka's family, all the bakers are women and girls like Dvoira. Bagel making is hard work. First special wheat is ground by hand on a stone into flour. Then it's sifted and mixed with water and "secret" stuff to make a dough. Then the dough is made into a long thick rope. Pieces are twisted off and made into a loop or figure 8. Then they are boiled in a big tub. The boiling is Dvoira's job. It's a hot job. She has to keep the fire going under the boiling pots all the time and be careful not to splash boiling water on herself when she puts the bagels in to boil. When they're done boiling, they're baked in an oven. That's when they turn golden. After that the bagels are strung on a rope and put in baskets to be sold or shipped to fairs and other places.

The holidays that come in the fall are called the high holidays, because they are especially important. Rosh Hoshana is the beginning of the Jewish New Year. We dip apples in honey to have a sweet year. For Rosh Hoshana Mama makes a special treat called taglach. She bakes balls of dough and then puts them in honey with ginger and pieces of the nuts I find. She makes enough to sell some to her milk customers. Since Maish left, we miss the gifts of meat or chickens he would bring. By selling her taglach Mama buys a chicken for our Rosh Hoshana dinner. This year she did something special. She carefully skinned the chicken before she cooked it. She was so careful that she kept the skin in one piece. Then she sewed up the cut part and stuffed the whole skin like she usually does the neck skin. She made the stuffing with flour and onions and chicken fat. When she was done it looked like an extra chicken! Papa said it was a miracle - Mama could turn one chicken into two.

Around Rosh Hoshana people talk a lot about sins. Papa says sins are bad things we do. The only thing that I can think of that I do that is bad is that I still sometimes wet my bed at night. But I don't do it on purpose and it seems to me a sin ought to be a bad thing you do on purpose and I really try not to wet my bed. On Rosh Hoshana, everybody in Karka goes along the shore of the lake where the water runs out in a stream and we do something called tashlich which I think means throwing away. We say prayers as we take the little pieces of lint from our pockets and throw them on the water. Papa says when we do this, we're throwing away our sins. I hear that in Smorgon people throw away little pieces of bread on the water. That's more fun because the fish and the ducks eat the bread. But in Karka we don't throw away even bread crumbs. I'm not sure how throwing lint or bread away will help me stop wetting my bed but it's worth trying so I do it.

A week after Rosh Hoshana comes Yom Kippur. On Yom

Kippur Jews don't eat anything for the whole day. It's called "the day of atonement" when Jews pray for forgiveness of their sins and forgive the sins of others. Little kids don't have to fast. That year, because I was seven, I decided I would fast like the rest of the family. The morning before Yom Kippur, Sarah and I walked through the forest gathering nuts. We filled a big pail. Then we walked to the Rabinowicz bagel bakery in Smorgon to walk home to Karka with Dvoira.

The bakery was busy selling bagels to be eaten before sundown. Of course the bakery is closed on the high holidays, Rosh Hoshana and Yom Kippur. So Dvoira gets to be home. And of course she doesn't get paid when she isn't working. Dvoira gave us each a fresh bagel to eat with the piece of cheese Mama gave us for lunch in the square while we waited for her. The shop closed at 2:00 p.m. but Dvoira had to clean up so we didn't get started home until about three. We took a basket of bagels home for our family and to sell to some of our neighbors in Karka. We would eat ours before sundown and keep the rest for when we broke our fast the next day at sundown. I put one in my pocket so I could eat it as soon as the sun went down and Yom Kippur was over.

On Yom Kippur this morning we all went to the big synagogue in Smorgon. Dvoira was still sleeping when we left and we knew she needed to rest. And Anna told us she was going to Vilna for a meeting on her day off. Papa just she shook his head. Jews aren't supposed to travel on Yom Kippur.

Only Mama and Papa went into the synagogue because you have to buy tickets for the high holidays and we couldn't afford tickets for the kids. Even Papa had to have a ticket although he helped the cantor to sing the prayers. Papa and Mama prayed a lot for the safety of Kate and Maish in America. Sarah and I prayed outside.

We played tag with the other kids outside the synagogue until the shamos came out and told us we were making too much noise. I wasn't feeling hungry until the kids decided to play a food game. We teased each other talking about what we wished we were eating. I said I wished I was eating a big piece of black bread with garlic rubbed over it and smeared with warm chicken fat schmaltz. Sarah said she wished she was eating a cold plate of beet borscht - a sweet red soup - with a glob of sour cream in the middle and pieces of cucumber floating on the top. I began thinking about the bagel I had in my pocket and how good it would taste right then.

In the afternoon Mama came out and we walked home to rest and wait for Papa to come home at sunset. Sarah and I tried to take a nap to keep our minds off of food. But we finally woke Dvoira and she teased us with a song about bagels and how good they tasted.

I was glad when Mama told me to go into Smorgon to find out when Papa would be home. I went to the synagogue but the shamos asked me for my ticket. I told him I just wanted to ask my Papa when he'll be home. "OK," he said, "you can go in, but if I catch you praying you'll be in trouble!" That was a joke he always played on us kids. I pretended to be worried and went in.

It was very noisy. Everyone was praying out loud, rocking back and forth - we call it dovening - but each one was going at his own speed - some fast, some slow, some loud, some soft, some high, some low. I asked Papa about it once and he said, "Jews believe each of us has a personal relationship to God. We come together on Shabbos and the holidays. The Rabbi and the cantor lead us. But each of us prays for ourselves without paying attention to the others around us."

It wasn't easy to find Papa because like a lot of the men he wore a big tallis, a prayer shawl, over his head and most of his body. But I found him at his favorite place by a wall.

"Mama wants to know when you'll be home," I said. I knew what he was going to say even before he said it.

"When I'll be home, I'll be home."

I said, in that case, I'd wait outside and walk home with him.

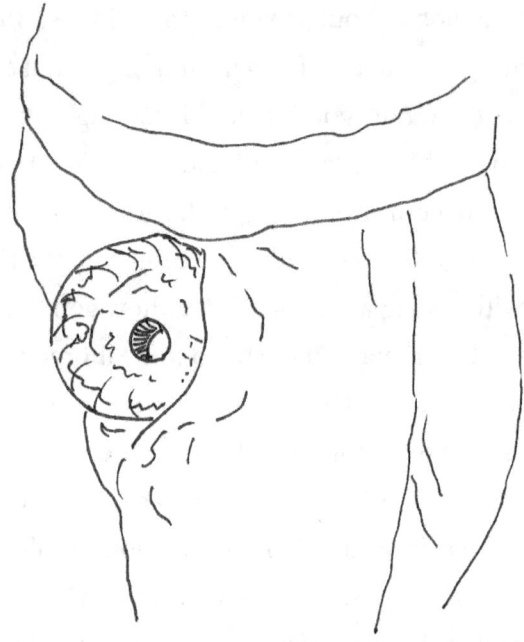

By now I was really hungry and I could feel that bagel in my pocket. The more I thought about it the hungrier I got. I decided maybe I wasn't quite old enough to fast for a whole day. But I couldn't eat it right there by the synagogue. So I began to walk away. I knew I would hear the shofar, the ram's horn, they blew to finish the Yom Kippur prayers. Pretty soon I was passing the railroad station. I went around the back so nobody would see me. There were some thick bushes near the track so I went in there to hide and eat my bagel. Just as I was pulling my bagel out of my pocket, someone put a hand over my mouth and held me tight.

"Quiet, don't say a word," a familiar voice said.

"Duvid Mendel! What are you doing here?" said another voice. "Did anyone see you come this way?"

I knew the voices. Imagine my bad luck. Hiding in the bushes were Avram and Dunya, my sister's friend. "Duvid Mendel," said Avram. "You have a bad habit of showing up in places you shouldn't be. How did you know to come here?"

I didn't know what to say, and before I could think up an excuse I told them the truth. "I got so hungry and I didn't want to eat by the synagogue, so I came down here where no one would see me." And I pulled out my bagel to show them.

They started laughing and I could see they were relieved. I'd been so scared I didn't realize there was a train coming through until it was almost there. Trains come through Smorgon all the time, but they only stop when someone is getting on or off. This train was stopping.

"Are you going someplace?" I asked, which was silly of me because I could see they didn't have any suitcases with them. And why would they be hiding?

Now the train was stopped and a woman was getting off. I remembered her from May Day. It was Chavera Froidela. She looked carefully around and then handed Avram a package and started to get back on the train.

"Chavera Froidela, do you know where my sister is?" I said. "We haven't heard from them since they left." She gave me a long look.

"Oh, I remember you, the little brother, the one they call der Kliegele, the smart one," she said. "I just left your sister in Chicago. She and Maish are fine. In fact in that package there's a letter for your family. I'm going back there when my business is done here. I'll see them soon."

"Thank you so much. What a wonderful surprise on Yom Kippur," I said. "Please tell them we miss them and Mama and Papa prayed for them."

"Just my luck," said Chavera Froidela, "to be here on Yom Kippur. I was hoping I could buy a Smorgon bagel at the station."

Her friends started laughing. "You're in luck," said Dunya, "this young man has brought you one."

Sadly I handed her the bagel.

"What a treasure," she said, pretending not to notice that the bagel looked like it had been in my pocket all day. "Thank you, my young friend. I'll tell your sister I saw her clever little brother." Then she was back on the train and she was gone with my bagel.

Avram opened the package and found Kate's letter. "My Mama will be so happy," I said. "We haven't heard from them since they left."

"Duvid Mendel," said Dunya, "you can't tell anyone how you got this letter. Just say that someone put it into your hands. You must not tell anyone you saw us or Chavera Froidela here."

Everybody seemed to be telling me things I couldn't tell anybody. But I promised I wouldn't tell anybody. "I'm sure your sister has sent letters in the mail," said Avram. "But the Czar's police have probably kept them. Wait and see, a whole bunch will show up at once all looking like they've been opened and read. We don't trust the mail. So we have our own system to stay in touch. Whenever anyone is coming back they carry letters with them."

Avram and Dunya went off through the woods from the station.

"Tseroo, Tseroo." I heard the stuttering trumpet sound of the shofar, the ram's horn that was blown at the end of the Yom Kippur service and ran back to the synagogue to find Papa standing outside.

"So, yingele," he said. "Did you make it through the whole day without eating?"

"Yes, Papa," I said, "I did."

"Nu," he said, "by fasting you have earned a blessing. We will have to find a suitable reward."

"I've already got my reward," I said, and I put the letter in his hands.

Papa's hands were trembling. "Where did you get this?" he said.

I couldn't lie to Papa so I said, "I promised not to tell."

He looked at me a long time, but all he said was. "Let's get home, Mama will be worried."

When we got home, Mama was not happy.

"Why are you so late?" she said. "Everyone has been home from the synagogue for a long time."

"Sha," said Papa. "We'll pray over the candles and the wine, say a prayer to bless our bread and then we'll eat and after that Duvid Mendel, who fasted all day for the first time in his life, has a surprise for us all."

As hungry as I was, I could hardly eat thinking about the letter from Kate and Maish. Finally, after we'd eaten our borsht and herring and boiled potatoes and shared some taglach Mama had saved for a treat, Papa said, "Duvid Mendel, it's time to share your surprise," and he handed me the letter. "It's from Kate and Maish,"

I said.

Mama, Dvoira and Sarah all spoke at once - "But how? Where? When?"

"Sha, Sha," said Papa. "Let's just say that Duvid Mendel has received a blessing for observing Yom Kippur."

I opened the letter. It was in Yiddish and I read it with a little help from Papa.

> Dear Mama, Papa and dear sisters and brother.
>
> You haven't answered our letters so we think you didn't get them. A friend has promised to give you this letter.
>
> We arrived safely in New York from the ship where friends from the movement met us. We stayed with them overnight and then they took us to a train to go to Chicago where Maish's uncle lives and some of our other friends from Smorgon are already working. We have jobs and a pleasant room near Lake Michigan, which is much bigger than our little lake in Karka. Chicago is not as big as New York but it's still very big - bigger by far than Vilna.
>
> Maish's uncle paints houses and Maish is working with him. I work in what they call a sweat shop here making ladies' clothes. It's hard work, but we make enough to save a little bit every week. We're sending you some money with this letter. We'll send more money when we can and when we find a safe way to send it. Anna, we hope you and our friends in the

movement are safe.

We love you and miss you all and can't wait until we are all together in America.

Kate and Maish

Out of the envelope fell a green bill that had 10 on the corners. "It's ten dollars," I said. "We're rich."

"Never mind rich," said Mama, snatching the money and putting it inside the top of her dress. "This is the start of the money we need to go to America."

"America," Papa said. "If we live, we'll see."

Two weeks later a bundle of letters arrived in the regular mail and we could see they'd been opened. That Friday, Anna came home for dinner. When she saw the letters she said, "The Czar has people who open the mail and read it. They think the people in the movement aren't smart enough to know that."

"But if the letters are written in Yiddish how can they read them?" I asked Anna.

"Think, my smart little brother," she said.

"They have people working for them who can read Yiddish?" I said.

Anna nodded. "We call them traitors to their people. That's why, little brother, you must be careful what you tell anyone."

"I know, I know," I said.

"See what comes from mixing in?" said Papa.

"After the revolution, we'll change all that. People will be free to speak or write anything they want," Anna said.

"After the revolution," Papa said, "it will be your friends who open people's mail."

Anna was about to answer him but Mama said, "Time to light the Sabbath candles and eat."

Eight
Revolution in Smorgon: January 1905

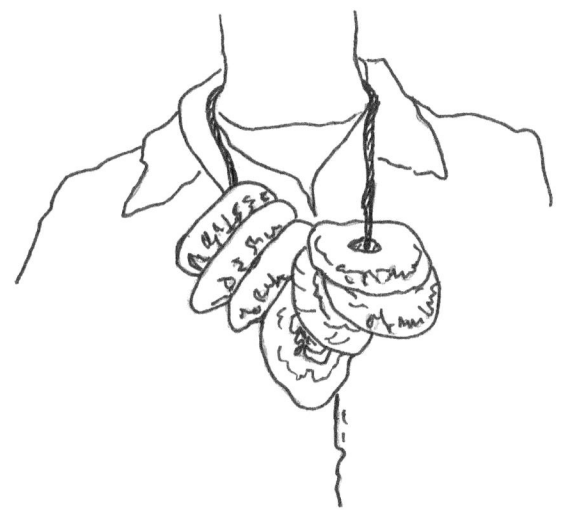

So that fall, when I was seven and a half we hardly ever saw Anna any more. She left her job in the bagel bakery and told Mama she was working for the movement all the time now. Papa probably knew that too but he pretended he didn't. In Yiddish we have a saying. When people want to pretend to not know something, we say they "make themselves not knowing." But Dvoira always knew how to get in touch with Anna and she could let us know Anna was still OK. And of course Sarah and I once more had to promise not to tell anybody what Anna was doing. What did they think we were, silly little kids?

The days were getting colder and shorter as winter got closer. It was light only a few hours each day. I missed Kate and Maish and the songs and stories when their friends came to our house. Anna would sneak in after dark for Friday night dinner sometimes but she never brought her friends. There wasn't even any of the old shouting that went with the arguments Anna and Kate and Papa used to have and I missed that too. I overheard Mama say to Papa, if we want to see Anna at all let's not argue about strikes and revolution.

Sometimes I saw Avram or Dunya on the streets and they nodded to me. There was ice now on the lake behind our house. Dvoira promised to teach Sarah and me to skate but she was only home on Shabbos and we didn't have any skates anyway.

We had a little excitement one day. Sarah and I and the other Karka kids were sliding on the ice on our little lake while a few kids were skating. Mostly we slid along next to the shore. But one of the little kids, Yankele, slid straight out to where the ice was thin. It cracked under him and he fell part way through. He didn't fall all the way in but his tusch, his bottom was in the water and he couldn't pull himself out. Everybody rushed to help him, but Sarah shouted out, "Don't get too close on the thin ice or you'll fall in too!"

It was kind of funny to think about it afterwards. There was Yankele with his tusch in the water crying loudly and waving his legs and arms on the ice. And all that did was break more of the ice. "Yankele, stay still for a minute and we'll get you out!" I shouted to him.

"Hurry up!" he sobbed. "My tusch is freezing!"

"Just take it easy!" called Sarah. "Hold your arms and legs still and we'll get you out!"

He kept crying but he stopped flailing around.

"Hold my legs!" I called to Sarah. I took off my coat and lay down on the ice while Sarah held onto my feet. Then I held one sleeve and threw the rest of the coat out to him so he could grab the other sleeve. When he had a good hold on it, we pulled him out.

Just as we got Yankele back to the shore, his mother came running up, screaming "Yankele, Yankele, my poor Yankele!" I thought she'd be happy we got him out. But she grabbed him and shook him and said, "Why do you always do things like this?" She gave him a hard potch on his wet tusch, which sent water flying in all directions, and dragged him off.

The kids were laughing and cheering for Sarah and me. They said we were heroes. When Mama heard what happened, she said, "I'm proud that you showed such quick thinking to get Yankele out of the water." Just the same she wouldn't let us play outside for a week and then only if we promised not to go near the lake.

There wasn't much of a Chanukah, or for that matter a Christmas either in 1904. Even in Smorgon we knew the Czar's army and navy were losing his war with Japan. It was getting hard for the trains to bring animal skins to make leather so the pay for the workers was cut even lower than it was before. It cost more for wheat to make bagels and people weren't buying as many. The people in Karka had trouble selling what they grew because people couldn't buy very much. Some families were giving up farming and moving into Smorgon to work in the factories and some who had family in America or the Holy Land were going there.

Oh, I forgot. I got a job. In fact I got two jobs. Can you guess my job? It was selling bagels at the train station! Dvoira got her boss, Mrs. Rabinowicz, to let me take bagels to the train station and sell them. The bagels were strung on a rope that I wore around my neck. After I finished my lessons with Papa I would go to the train station to find out if any trains were going to stop there that evening. Then I would go to the bakery to get the bagels and go back to the station to wait for the train.

If people were waiting to meet anybody or getting on or off the train I would call out, "Buy my wonderful bagels! Smorgon invented bagels and these are the best in Smorgon, made with a secret family recipe! Buy my fresh cheap delicious Smorgon bagels!" I learned to say that in Yiddish, Lithuanian, Belarussian and Russian. And of course I could give people the right change when they paid me.

When the train left I would take the money and the leftover bagels back to the bakery and get my pay. A couple of times I got on the train to sell my bagels to the people who weren't getting off, but usually the train man chased me out. I couldn't run too fast with those bagels around my neck. I didn't get paid much and I gave most of it to Mama, but it was something to do and it made up for the Chanukah gelt I didn't get that year.

I liked that job. But I didn't get to keep it very long. Partly that's because of my second job. My second job was a secret. Dvoira told me that sometimes when someone bought a bagel from me they would say, "What a clever boy you are!" in Yiddish. Then I had to answer, "I'm the smartest boy in Smorgon." After that they would pretend to give me a hug and put a small package in my coat. Or sometimes Dvoira would put a package in my coat and the people would take it out when they hugged me. I knew this had something to do with the movement. But to me it was a game and I liked the idea that Dvoira trusted me and I was playing a grown-up game. Dvoira also told me to keep my eyes open and tell her if anybody unusual got off or on the train. I was supposed to tell her if any soldiers or policemen got off or any people that didn't seem like they belonged in Smorgon.

One day when I was selling my bagels a train from Minsk stopped at the station. I'd just finished selling a bagel when I heard a voice say, "What a clever boy you are."

I knew it was Anna from her voice. She had just gotten off the train. But I still answered, "I'm the smartest boy in Smorgon." She gave me a really strong hug and a kiss on my cheek. And she whispered softly in my ear, "I miss you." Then she got back on the train to go on to Vilna before I could say anything else.

When I got back to the bakery Dvoira put her arm around my shoulders and we walked around in back. I gave her the envelope Anna had put in my coat. She opened it and read it. And then she said, as if she were talking to herself, "It's starting."

"What's starting?" I said.

"Never mind," she said. "Duvid Mendel, I can't leave here until my work is done, tonight. But I need you to take this letter to Dunya. Go to the side door of the church. Stay in the shadows so people won't see you. Knock on the door like this. Three times, then two times, then three again. Can you remember that?"

"Three, then two, then three." I said.

"Clever boy," she said. "Give the letter only to Dunya, but don't stay there. Go right home."

"What was starting?" I wondered as I ran from shadow to shadow. Smorgon had no lights in the streets like Vilna or Minsk did, so it was easy to move through the shadows. I moved quietly around the dark church to the side door. I knocked softly as Dvoira said I should. Three, then two then three. Nothing happened. I was about to knock again when a quiet voice said, "Who knocks at this door?" I didn't know what to say. Then I said, "The smartest boy in Smorgon." I heard some quiet laughing and the door opened a crack and a hand came out, pulled me in and shut the door behind me. It was dark. Someone lit a candle and then I was glad to see Dunya and Avram. I had a feeling there were others there too, but I couldn't see them.

I gave the letter to Dunya. "Dvoira told me to bring this to you right away." She took the letter and Avram held the candle close to it so they could read it.

"It's starting," he said.

"It's starting," answered Dunya.

"What's starting?" I said.

"Never mind," Dunya said. "You'll know soon enough. You have to go home now. Can you find your way back to Karka by yourself?"

"Of course," I said.

"And Duvid Mendel," said Avram –

"I know, I know," I said. "Don't tell anybody."

They both laughed. "That too," he said. "But I want you to know you did something very important tonight."

I slipped out of the door and rushed home. I would walk a ways and run a while but always quietly. Mama and Papa would be worried because I was so late. It was very dark and very cold and a steady snow was falling. My breath made clouds as I moved as fast as I could through the snow. I saw a patch of ice and I slid on it but there was a rock under the snow and I fell over it as it stopped my slide. I didn't hurt myself. But the snow got into my coat where I fell and I started feeling cold and wet. By the time I got to the door of my house I was shivering and shaking with the cold. Mama heard me coming. She opened the door and let me inside.

"Where have you been? You must be meshugenah to be playing in the snow in the dark?" shouted Papa.

"I had errands from the bagel bakery when I got back there," I said, staying as close to the truth as possible.

"That's it!" Papa said. "No more bagel selling, no more errands. From now on after we finish the lessons with the other boys there will be special lessons for you. My son will be a scholar not a pedlar at the railroad station."

Mama handed us each a hot glass of tea as she got me out of my cold wet clothes and she put a warm blanket around me and sat me in front of the oven where it was warm.

I was sad about not getting to sell bagels any more but as it turned out it didn't make much difference anyway. It was starting.

That night after we were sent to bed Sarah pulled my hair and said she was going to keep doing it until I told her what really happened.

"It's starting," I said, deciding it was safe to tell her that much.

"What's starting?" she said.

"Ouch, stop pulling my hair. That's all I can tell you," I said. "They made me promise not to tell. But you'll find out soon enough."

The next morning we both found out what was starting. Every house had a red paper stuck to it.

Hundreds killed in St. Petersburg on bloody Sunday.

General Strike! All Workers leave your jobs.

Down with Autocracy!

Workers and peasants of Smorgon unite!

The revolution is starting!

The red papers were everywhere. It was the revolution that was starting! Sarah and I looked at each other. What does that mean? Anna had brought the news to Smorgon on Tuesday. Now it was Wednesday morning. We took the paper to Papa. Mama wasn't home yet from selling her milk. But Papa had his prayer shawl over his shoulders and was deep in his morning prayers. We had to wait for him to finish.

As soon as he was done, we both were on him. Sarah pushed the paper in front of him. We both talked at once. "Papa, it's starting," I said.

"The paper says people were killed in St. Petersburg," said Sarah. "But why? Who killed them Papa?"

Papa took the paper from Sarah and stared at it. "What is this? The whole world is meshugenah. It's gone mad. God protect us from such madness."

"What's happening Papa?" we said. "What should we do?"

Papa didn't have time to answer. There was a loud banging on our door and we could hear our neighbors' voices. "Rabbi, tell us what this means," said Reb Yussel, waving the red paper. "Tell us, tell us, Rabbi. What should we do?" They were all shouting.

Papa seemed to find himself in all the noise. He raised his hand for them to be quiet. "Come into the Shul, the prayer house, and we will pray together," he said. "Then we will all go back to our homes and stay there with our families and wait to see what happens. Maybe nothing will happen."

"But Papa," I said. "It's starting."

"So it will start without us," said Papa. And he took Sarah and me by the hand and led us into the Shul and our neighbors all followed. Papa led a short service and prayed for peace and calm. Then he told everyone to go home and do their work.

As we were coming out Mama came back. "I had to give my milk to my first few customers and come home," she said. "The students have left the Yeshivas. People are out in the streets. Everyone is trying to make sense of what is happening. The Smorgon police are telling everybody to go to work as usual. They say there was no killing. It's just a rumor."

At noon Dvoira came home. "It's started!" she shouted as she ran up to the door. "The revolution is starting!"

Mama made Dvoira sit down and gave her a glass of tea and piece of black bread with butter. Dvoira took a sip of the tea and a bite of the bread.

"A message came to the leaders here. Anna brought it," she said.

"Anna?" Mama said. "She's here? Where is she?"

"She went on to bring the message to Vilna. She'll be back for the meeting tomorrow."

"What message, what meeting?" Sarah said.

Papa said quietly, "What has our Anna gotten herself into now? What can we do with such a daughter?"

"She's a leader, Papa," said Dvoira. "When she speaks people listen. They call her Anna, the Starke - the strong one."

"And where is this leader Anna leading us now?" said Papa. "Is she leading us all to Siberia?"

Mama said, "Dvoirale, tell us what is going on. Yankle Laib, let's hear what she has to say."

"Last Sunday, January 9, in St. Petersburg, thousands of students, workers and farmers came to the Czar's palace with a petition," Dvoira told us. "The petition asked for simple things that people in other countries have. More pay, shorter work days. An elected government. Schools. Freedom."

"But the Czar wouldn't talk to them. He ordered his soldiers and the Cossacks to shoot them. Hundreds of people were killed and many more were hurt. So now there will be a strike all over the Czar's empire and a revolution."

"Even in Smorgon?" asked Sarah?

"Especially in Smorgon. But also in Minsk, in Vilna, in Warsaw, in Moscow. In every city and shtetl. And we're not just striking for better pay and shorter work days. Now we won't stop the strike until the Czar gives in and working people have their freedom all over Russia," said Dvoira. "This morning the leaders came to each place people were working and each school to tell us what happened and to tell us about the strike. People left their work and their schools. They're shouting in the streets 'Long live freedom!' and 'Down with Autocracy!'"

"What's 'Autocracy'?" I asked.

"It's a word to say 'Down with'" said Papa.

"The Czar and his soldiers rule over all the people. They make up bad rules. They take everything we have and keep it for themselves. And if we complain they put us in jail. They won't give us freedom. That's Autocracy," said Dvoira. "So we say, 'Down with Autocracy. Long live freedom.'"

"And what will you be free to do? Free to starve, free to get shot by the Czar's soldiers, free to be sent away to Siberia?" said Papa.

"Free to think, to speak our minds, to vote for our leaders," Dvoira answered.

"Free to continue to live our lives as Jews, as God expects us to?" said Papa.

"Or not. We will all be the same, Jew, Christian and Moslem, all citizens of Russia with the same freedom and the same rights," she said. "We will each live as we choose to live?"

"For hundreds of years we Jews have managed without that kind of freedom. And still we live our lives as Jews. Now your freedom will make us leave our home and go to a strange land," he said.

"No Papa, The revolution will let us stay here. Anna says Kate and Maish can come back and we can all live here. There will be schools for Sarah and Duvid Mendel. Maybe I can go to school too. It's not too late for me to go to school," she said.

"A school for girls to learn to make revolutions? And when does this new world begin?" he said softly.

"Tomorrow morning," she said. "At 6:00 a.m. on Vilna Street in Smorgon there will a big rally. That's when it will begin. And Anna will be one of the speakers. I'm so proud that my sister is leading the revolution in Smorgon. My sister Anna."

"The Starke!" Sarah and I said together.

Papa gave me his look. "Errands, you had last night, Duvid Mendel, yes?"

"Yes, Papa," I barely whispered.

"And you got one errand at the railroad station? From a certain revolutionary leader, a certain Starke?"

"Papa, I –" I started but I didn't know what to say.

He held up his hand to stop me anyway. "No more errands for this boy. You hear me, Dvoira. Tell your very important sister no more errands for him. Tomorrow we will all go to this meeting that begins a new free world for us all. And this 'clever boy' will stay at my side. And whatever else happens there will be no more errands for him."

Workers in the leather factories usually started their work at five o'clock in the morning. But there was no work that Thursday morning. The meeting was supposed to start at six a.m. But by four o'clock the streets were full of people. The barbers, the bagel bakers, the leather workers even the merchants formed rows and marched through streets which were lit up by the lanterns or torches everyone was carrying. Jews, Christians, Gypsies, Moslems all were in the streets. The Jewish farmers from Karka and their families joined the others with Papa leading them.

At 6:00 a.m. the meeting started. Dvoira said she heard there were three thousand people there.

They had made a wooden platform in the square at the end of Vilna Street. We were way back in the crowd so I couldn't see much but I heard the sound of music- mandolins and balalaikas and then someone started a song. I knew the voice. It was Dunya. I heard the song before too. Maish used to sing it. It was called the Warshavyarka. The whole crowd began to sing with Dunya.

"To the bloody battle, sacred and just, march forward working people!"

I started to sing too but I felt Papa's strong hand on my neck and I stopped.

There were two speakers. First was Comrade Levy and then Anna. Comrade Levy was a poet from another shtetl called Igumen and a friend of Maish's. I couldn't see a lot because of all the big people around me. I tried to climb up on a wall so I could see better but Papa pulled me down and kept me right next to him. He had me by one hand and Sarah by the other. Comrade Levy spoke for the students and told the story of Bloody Sunday and how the Czar had his soldiers and Cossacks shoot the people who came peacefully to ask him for their freedom. He said that the workers and students would lead all the people of the Czar's lands to freedom. Then he read a Yiddish poem he had written. I don't remember it all and I didn't understand a lot of what I heard. It was about hard work, poor people starving, and how everybody wanted a better world to live in. When he finished, everyone cheered.

Now it was Anna's turn. She reminded people of how hard they worked and how they had to go to work before their children were awake and come home after they were already asleep. She talked about how the Czar stirred up people to hate each other instead of hating him and the people who made their lives so miserable. She said children as young as nine or ten were working instead of being in school. She said Russia was the most backward country in Europe. Sometimes Anna spoke in Yiddish and sometimes she spoke in Russian. I understood Anna because I'd heard all the things she was talking about in the arguments she and Kate had with Papa.

As she finished, Anna shouted to the crowd, "Have you suffered enough?"

"Enough!" they shouted back.

"Do you want your freedom?" she shouted.

"Freedom!" the crowd roared.

"Today Smorgon belongs to its people," she said, "and tomorrow all of Russia will belong to the people. Down with Autocracy!" she shouted.

And then they began to chant, "Enough! Freedom!" and "Down with Autocracy!"

"The revolution has begun," said Anna. "We will not stop until we have won our freedom."

Dunya and the musicians started singing the Warshavyarka again and the crowd marched away in rows singing it. All that day until 9:00 o'clock at night people marched through the streets shouting slogans and singing.

Papa, still holding Sarah and me by the hand, led the people of Karka home where our neighbors continued to shout slogans and sing in the street. He made Dvoira come home with us, even though she wanted to keep marching with the Bagel bakers.

Mama made a lunch for us of beet borsht, boiled potatoes, herring and black bread. And Papa got out his bottle of schnappes and had a drink. He kept the bottle out and served some of the men who came to talk about what was happening.

For Sarah and me and the other kids it was like a big holiday. We marched around and played at fighting the soldiers of the Czar. Some of us were Cossacks and we galloped around on broomstick horses and chased the others. Sarah pretended she was Anna and she made a speech and we carried her around on our shoulders.

That night Anna came with Avram, Dunya and others she said were from the committee. They were on their way to a meeting in the woods where they would plan what to do next.

Mama wanted her to stay but she said tomorrow the committee will take over the police station and the mayor's office. Each factory and workshop will be taken over by its workers. And Smorgon will join with committees from Vilna, Minsk and the other cities and shtetls to get rid of the Czar's police and soldiers.

"How can you take over the police station?" I said.

"We are many and they are few," she said, "They're hiding now."

Papa said, "Nothing good can come from this. The Czar is too strong. You'll all be arrested and sent to Siberia or worse. Anna, you must stop this nonsense now."

"We can't stop now," she said. "We won't stop until we've won."

She kissed us all, even Papa, and then she and her friends were gone to the woods.

It turned out Papa was partly right. Overnight, the Governor came on a train from Vilna with 300 soldiers and a lot of Cossacks on their horses. There was shooting the next morning. They arrested over 100 people and kept the committee from holding an even bigger meeting than the day before. They kept the people off the streets and ordered them to go back to work.

For the next week there was a war of shooting and of paper. The committee put up a paper called, "The Fall of Autocracy and our Tasks." The governor put up one that said, "Warning. Stop the strike or the strictest measures will be taken."

But the working people didn't go back to work and they stayed on strike. More people were arrested. Some were shot or beaten up by the soldiers. The Cossacks rode through the streets chasing people back into their houses. Finally the Governor put Smorgon and the bigger cities "under protected guard" and ordered everybody to go back to work or be arrested. More soldiers were sent into every town including Smorgon.

During that week we heard nothing from Anna. Dvoira begged Papa to let her go to find out what was happening to her. Papa was worried but he wouldn't let Dvoira go. He was afraid she would be arrested or hurt.

That night there was a knock on the door. Mama opened it and it was Vanya, Dunya's brother who was my age. Quickly she let him in. "My father sent me to bring you bad news," he said. "The Cossacks found where the committee was meeting in the woods. They arrested Anna, Comrade Levy, my sister Dunya and most of the others."

"Didn't Avram's bears scare them away?" I said.

"Avram got away but the Cossacks shot the bears," said Vanya.

"How did you find out?" said Papa.

"The police came to the church for my Papa, Father Vasily. They were going to arrest him too but a big crowd gathered around the church. Finally the police left, but they told my Papa if he leaves the church they will put him in jail."

"So maybe they will come here too," said Papa.

"No," said Dvoira. "Anna has been careful. She doesn't use her real name."

"But tomorrow I must go to the jail to see Anna," Papa said.

"They're not there," said Vanya. "They've taken them to jail in Vilna."

"Did anyone see you come here?" I said.

"Of course not, "Vanya said. "You think you're the only smart kid around here?"

That night I had a dream. Vanya and I were running through the woods. But we weren't boys we were bear cubs. We were running with other forest animals, rabbits and deer and foxes. As we ran we shouted, "Down with Autocracy!" The other animals shouted, "Down with Autocracy!" Somebody was behind us and shooting at us. It was the Cossacks.

"Follow me," I called to Vanya, and I ran into a cave in the forest. We were safe from the Cossacks but I could hear voices and I saw a light far ahead in the cave. Vanya and I quietly moved through the cave toward the light. From the shadows we could see a large opening. It was lit by lamps and torches. Anna and Dunya and Avram were there and so were Kate and Maish and some others of their friends. But they were dressed like the police and they wore red arm bands.

The governor was tied up like a prisoner and so were some bosses. Papa and two other rabbis sat at a high table. Father Vasily was in front of them and he was saying, "So I want you to find the Autocracy guilty and send them to Siberia."

Papa and the other rabbis put their heads together for a few minutes and it got very quiet. Finally Papa banged on the table with his shoe. Then the three rabbis together said, "We have decided that we shouldn't mix in."

The next thing I knew it was morning.

Nine

The Kaziuk Fair and the Trial: March 1905

Every town and city around where we lived has at least one fair every year. And the biggest of all is the Kaziuk Fair in Vilna. At fairs people come from all over to buy and sell things that they make and grow. And there are wonderful foods and entertainers. I knew about the Kaziuk Fair because my sisters got to go there to sell the things they made on their jobs. One year Kate brought me a heart-shaped cookie with my name on it from the fair.

I tried to think of ways of getting to go to the Kaziuk Fair but as it turned out it was Anna's trouble that actually got me there.

After she and the others were arrested, there were always soldiers in the street in Smorgon and Cossacks would ride through Karka almost every day. Dvoira went back to her job in the bagel bakery. We heard that Anna and the others were in jail in Vilna and that there would be a trial.

Sometimes people who get arrested by the Czar's police don't even get a trial. They just get sent away to icy Siberia or worse yet they just disappear. This time there would be a trial. There were still strikes and fighting all over our district and the Governor wanted everybody to know what would happen to people who started a revolution.

"Oi, Vey, what will be with our Anna now?" Mama cried out when she heard about the trial.

"The Governor is going to make an example of them," said Papa. "There will be a public trial and then they will be found guilty and sent far away to Siberia."

"Is Siberia very far away?" I asked.

"It's far, far away. Some parts of it are very cold. And it is so far that anybody who tried to escape and come back would die on the way," said Papa.

"The Czar sends criminals there," said Dvoira.

"But Anna and her friends aren't criminals," I said.

Dvoira said, "To the Czar they are worse than criminals. They're fighting against the Czar."

"Yankle Laib," Mama said. "You need to go to Vilna for this trial. Anna needs to know we care about her."

"How can I go?" said Papa. "The police will arrest me too. And nothing will help them. Anna knew this could happen."

One evening after dinner there was a knock on the door. "My Papa, Father Vasily, wants your Papa to come and see him," said Vanya as soon as I opened the door.

I begged Papa to let me go with him. He was keeping me pretty close to him anyway so it wasn't hard to get him to let me go.

Father Vasily let us in when we got to his house. I'd never been in Vanya's house before. It was next to the church. That's because his Papa was the priest. It was a lot bigger than ours and there were pictures of saints on the walls. I knew they were saints because they had rings over their heads.

Father Vasily and Papa went into a room with shelves of books on the walls. Vanya and I pretended to play in the next room but we could hear what they were saying. Father Vasily said that the trial for Anna and Dunya would be in Vilna the beginning of March. "I think you and I should go to the trial," he said.

"I want to go so Anna can see we care about her. But how can we go?" said Papa. "The soldiers will arrest you. Probably they'll arrest me too."

"I've thought of a plan," said Father Vasily. "The Kaziuk Fair will be going on in Vilna at that time. It's the biggest fair of the year. That's why the trial will be held then. Thousands of people will be there for the fair. The Governor wants everybody to know how people who start revolutions are punished. Wagon loads of leather and bagels go there from Smorgon every year to be sold at the fair. You and I can dress as wagon drivers and drive wagons to Vilna for the fair. Once we are there, we'll go to the trial."

Papa stroked his beard. "Hmm, wagon drivers? Why not? My Dvoira is supposed to go there with a wagon of bagels from her bakery. I'm sure her boss, Malka Rabinowicz, could use a driver, especially one who would work for no pay."

"Yes, and I know a man who owns a leather factory," said Father Vasily. "He'll let me drive one of his wagons."

Vanya and I hugged each other. The Kaziuk Fair. We heard

stories about it but we never thought we actually could get there. The dancing bears from Smorgon would be there and all kinds of wonderful things to see and hear and taste. But how could we get our fathers to let us come along?

When the door opened and Papa and Father Vasily came out, Vanya grabbed his father's hand. "Oh, Papa," sobbed Vanya. "I'm so worried about Dunya, my wonderful sister. I want to see her at the trial."

"Me too," I cried, trying to make tears run down my face, "Poor Anna. I have to see Anna."

Vanya's father said, "You know, Rabbi, having a boy sitting on the driver's seat next to each of us is not such a bad idea. Wagon drivers often have a boy to look after the horses."

"Many rabbis from the whole district come to Vilna at the time of the fair. We have meetings then. My son can meet the important rabbis who may have some ideas about his education," said Papa.

"And after all, Rabbi, they're so worried about their sisters," Father Vasily said, and he winked at Vanya.

So it was settled without even a fight. Except for Mama. In ordinary times it's a long and dangerous trip. The road goes through the dark forest in places. Bandits could be there or Cossacks.

"You would take my baby, my Duvidel, on such a dangerous trip? How could you think of such a thing?"

"Mama!" I protested. "I'm not a baby! I'm big now. I can take care of myself and help Papa on the wagon."

I thought my dream trip was done for. Usually Mama wins this kind of argument. But to my surprise, Papa really wanted me to go.

"The boy will be on the wagon seat with Dvoira and me and there will be many wagons going to Vilna," said Papa. "He's old enough now to see something of the world outside of Karka and Smorgon. Besides perhaps I can show the other rabbis what a clever boy he is."

Mama shook her head but she could see Papa had made up his mind.

Dvoira talked to Mrs. Rabinowicz, her boss, the next day. "No pay?" she said. Of course, Papa could drive a wagon for her.

In Lithuania the most important holiday is March 4, St. Kasimir's Day. Kaziuk means little Kasimir. So the Kaziuk Fair is held on St. Kasimir's Day. But Jews are very important buyers and sellers at the fair. In 1905 March 4 was on a Saturday, and Jews aren't supposed to buy and sell on Saturday. So the Kaziuk Fair was on Friday that year.

That meant that we had to start out very early Thursday morning because it was about 50 miles to Vilna from Smorgon and it would take us nine or ten hours to get there.

For a week before the fair, all the bagel bakers in town were busy night and day baking bagels. That Thursday morning we were up very early to get to the bakery to help load the wagons. Papa had borrowed a wagon driver's clothes for the trip. We all laughed after he got dressed.

"So how do I look?" said Papa.

"By you, you're a wagon driver, but by me you're no wagon driver," said Mama. He didn't look at all like a Rabbi either.

When we got to the bagel bakery Dvoira and the other girls who worked there were already bringing the baskets of steaming bagels out to the wagons. The bagels were strung on rings of rope. The rings were put in big baskets covered with white cloths to keep the dust of the road off them.

I rode on the wagon seat behind the horses between Papa and Dvoira. By the time we passed the street of the leather factories there must have been thirty wagons of bagels. There was a long line of wagons full of leather and shoes, belts and coats made of leather waiting to follow us. We saw Father Vasily dressed in his driver's clothes and he looked funny too. He waved to us.

Vanya called to me, "See you at the fair!"

It was still dark so lanterns were hung on the wagons so we could see where we were going. When we got out on the Vilna Road, farmers came out to see us go by. The whole road smelled like bagels and the white clothes flapped in the wind above the wagons. Ahead of us we could see the lanterns on many other wagons and when we looked back there were wagons as far as we could see. Dvoira and I guessed all the wonderful things that were in the wagons.

As the sun came up we could see the fields we passed had patches of snow, and there was nothing growing yet because it was still winter. Sometimes we would pass bare apple trees. Sometimes the road went through the dark forests but with so many wagons there was not much danger. Sometimes we had to cross narrow bridges and wait if a wagon was coming in the other direction. But most of the wagons were headed toward Vilna just like us. We passed a pretty big shtetl called Ashmiany and there were more wagons coming into the road there.

Mama had packed a basket of food and when the sun was high in the sky we ate our lunch of black bread and cheese and drank some milk. Sometimes I would get off and run along the side of the wagon. It couldn't move very fast because of the heavy load of bagels it carried and all the wagons moving slowly ahead of it.

I got tired in the afternoon and laid down in the wagon on top of the white cloth over the bagels.

Bouncing in the wagon, with the strong smell of the bagels all around me, I had a strange dream.

I dreamed that I was at the trial. There were Anna and Dunya and the others. They were all dressed like wagon drivers. But the judge was a fierce looking eagle who kept opening his beak and screaming, "Guilty! Guilty!" Instead of people in the court room there were bears, and every time the eagle judge screamed, "Guilty! Guilty!" they would get up and dance and shout, "Not Guilty! Not Guilty!" But then strange creatures came into the court room. The top of each one was a Cossack and the bottom was a horse. The eagle-judge screamed, "Guilty! Off to Siberia!" The Cossack horses grabbed Anna and the others and dragged them out of the courtroom shouting, "Guilty! Off to Siberia!"

But, outside the courthouse, the road was blocked with wagons full of bagels. The bears came out and started throwing rings of bagels around the necks of the Cossack Horses. Vanya and Sarah were there with me. Papa and Father Vasily were standing back to back on top of a wagon driver's seat. Papa was saying a Hebrew Prayer and Father Vasily was praying in a language I didn't know. Vanya and Sarah and I yelled for Anna and Dunya and the others to climb into the wagon. And then Papa and Father Vasily drove the wagon up into the sky and away from the court house.

That's when I woke up. Our bagel wagon was stopped with all the other bagel wagons. We were in a huge field. Around us I could see many houses and buildings. I knew it must be Vilna.

Papa was up with the horses. "So did you have a good nap, Duvid Mendel?" he called. "Time now to help me with the horses."

Papa and I unhitched the horses. Then we helped Dvoira and

the other girls unload the bagels. All the bagel wagons were doing the same thing. There was a place to tie up our horses and Papa sent me to tie up ours and give them some food and water. Meanwhile, the unloaded wagons were tipped backwards so the wagon shafts were sticking high in the air. The rings of bagels were hung on the shafts so people could see where to come to buy the Smorgon bagels.

That night Dvoira and the other bakery girls slept under the wagon. Papa took me into Vilna. We had to walk for a long time until we came to the great Synagogue. There were many other shuls in the area. Papa said they call this part of Vilna the Shulhayf.

Next to the great synagogue was a big house. Papa and I went around to the side door of the house and knocked there. A servant opened the door and when he saw how Papa was dressed he thought we were beggars. But Papa said, "Please, you should be so kind to tell Rabbi Eliezer that Rabbi Yankle Laib Gutman from Karka near Smorgon is here to see him."

The servant looked a bit doubtful but he said, "Wait here." In a few minutes the servant came back and said, "Please come in. The Rabbi is in with a group of Rabbis but he'll come out soon."

We were taken into a room with beautiful furniture. A picture on the wall was of a rabbi with a full white beard. "Duvid Mendel, This is a picture of the great Saadya Gaon. Many years ago he was the chief rabbi here. Jews came from all over the world to hear him talk and to get his answers to their questions."

When the door opened Rabbi Eliezer came in and looked very surprised when he saw Papa. He burst out laughing and said, "Shalom! My dear friend Yankle Laib, what has happened to you that you are dressed this way? Are those Karka farmers treating you so badly?"

Papa laughed. "No," he said. "My daughter Anna is one of those on trial just now and I thought it best to come to Vilna as a wagon driver. This is my son Duvid Mendel."

Rabbi Eliezer patted my head and said, "Shalom, Duvid Mendel. How do you do?"

"Shalom Aleichem, Rabbi," I said.

"Tell me about your daughter, which one is it? I remember you have a lot of daughters," he said.

"It's my sister, Anna," I said. "They call her the Starke."

Papa gave me his evil eye look.

"She's a good girl. A bright one. But she's mixed up with these rebels and was arrested as a leader," he said.

"Your little Anna is the one they call the Starke?" said Rabbi Eliezer. "How old could she be to be a leader already?"

"Old enough to be in a lot of trouble. She's almost 19 years old," said Papa.

They went on talking about how things were changing. How the young people had all these new ideas. My mind began to wander and pretty soon I noticed a pretty glass dish with candy in it.

The rabbi kept right on talking to Papa as he picked up the dish and held it in front of me.

"And how about this yingele?" he asked. "Is he also a rebel?"

I took a red piece of candy that had sugar on the outside and was soft and fruity on the inside.

"We call him the smart one," said Papa. "Already he can read in Hebrew and Yiddish and even a little Russian. And I have started him on the Torah. He will be a scholar, this one."

I'd never heard Papa brag about me before. I liked it.

"Maybe there will be a place for such a bright young fellow in our Yeshiva when he's ready," said Rabbi Eliezer.

"If we live, we'll see," said Papa.

"Of course," he answered, "If we live we'll see."

Then he gave a little laugh and he said, "Rabbi Yankle Laib. I've just thought of a wonderful joke we can play on the other rabbis. Just now I was having a discussion about the Torah with several very learned rabbis who are in Vilna for the fair. We were having an argument over a particularly difficult question. Half are on one side and half on the other. They're waiting now to hear what I think about the question. Come in now and we'll have some fun with them."

We went into a larger room. There were about 25 rabbis there, all arguing when we came in the room. Twenty-five arguing rabbis can make a lot of noise.

"Excuse me for keeping you waiting," he said. "I had some business with this wagon driver and his son. Now what was the question we were discussing?"

One rabbi pointed to a part in the Torah and repeated the question they were arguing about and said, "So now Rabbi Eliezer you heard what we think. Now we want to hear your answer?"

"I'm really surprised at you," said Rabbi Eliezer. "You can't agree on such a simple question. Even this simple wagon driver could answer that question. Wagon driver tell them the answer."

"My Papa–" I started to say. But Papa's hand went over my mouth.

"I need to read over the Torah part but I forgot my eye glasses," said my Papa. "Duvid Mendel please read this for me."

I was surprised he said that. Papa doesn't wear glasses. I didn't have any idea what it was about, but I read the Hebrew with no trouble, rocking back and forth as Papa had taught me to do.

The rabbis nodded their heads. "The driver's little son reads Hebrew beautifully," I heard one whisper.

Then Papa began to speak. He talked about this great rabbi and that great rabbi and told a story that the rabbis seemed to find very interesting. Then he answered so simply and so wisely that all the Rabbis applauded when he finished.

"Amazing, a simple wagon driver, but so wise," one said. "Amazing," said another.

"Now what were you going to say, yingele," Rabbi Eliezer said to me.

"My Papa is Rabbi Yankle Laib Gutman, Rabbi of Karka near Smorgon," I said proudly.

Everybody laughed when they knew that we played a joke on them.

That night we had a wonderful dinner in Rabbi Eliezer's house. After dinner there were more arguments among the Rabbis and I could see the other rabbis thought my father knew a lot. And more than once he told them what a clever little boy I was. I couldn't believe it. After a while I fell asleep and Papa carried me to a room in the basement of the great synagogue where we could sleep.

The next morning Papa gave Rabbi Eliezer a gift of Smorgon bagels and I had one with a glass of milk for my breakfast. Then we went back to the fair.

It was a cold morning but sunny and the fair was coming to life. We found Dvoira helping to set up the bagels to be sold. Papa left me with her while he went to find Father Vasily. She gave me a hug and I told her about the joke Rabbi Eliezer had played on the other rabbis.

I told her how Papa had me read the Hebrew. "Papa told all the rabbis how smart I am," I told her.

"He wants you to get into a Yeshiva and become a rabbi," she said. "Is that what you want?"

"No," I said. "I want to go to America and be rich."

Dvoira laughed. "More likely you'll be poor in America too."

"Poor in America? Nobody's poor in America," I said.

Dvoira just laughed.

"So let's go see the fair." It was Vanya. He'd come back with his Papa and mine.

"Father Vasily and I are going to find out about the trial," said Papa. "You and Vanya can walk around and see the fair but you must stay together and you must come back here every hour or so to make sure Dvoira knows you're OK. We'll be back by lunch time. Here are a few kopeks to spend."

Papa gave me 3 kopeks. I didn't tell Papa I had 5 kopeks I had saved up to bring with me to the fair. I wanted to buy something nice for Mama.

Vanya and I said goodbye to Dvoira and started on our adventure. Lots of different people live in Vilna. And we saw so many kinds at the fair. Vanya and I played a game. I would guess what the people were and he would tell me their religion.

I saw Lithuanians. He said they were mostly Catholics. I thought some people were Polish. He said they were Catholics too. The Russians and Belarussians were Orthodox like Vanya and his father, Vanya told me. He guessed which ones were Jews. I told him what kind. There are also Karaites who believe they are Jews too. We saw Tartars and Turks who Vanya said are Moslems. There were lots of blond haired Finns and Estonians. Vanya says they are Lutherans.

And there are many Gypsies. We didn't know about their religion. But besides those people there were people from far away who came to buy and sell. Some of them looked and dressed in ways that Vanya and I had never seen before. A few even had dark brown skins. We thought maybe they were sailors off ships. We imagined that they were from exciting faraway places.

We saw gypsy fortune tellers and Chinese jugglers. We stopped to watch them for a while. A group of Russians were playing accordions and doing wild dances where they got down so low they were almost on the ground with their boots flying out in front of them. Vanya could do it but when I tried I kept falling. A Russian came over and showed me how to move my legs without falling.

We found a group of Jewish klezmer musicians and I showed Vanya a Jewish dance called a Scher that I learned from my cousin Yussele.

There was food from everywhere and the smells made us hungry. Vanya bought a Polish sausage but it wasn't kosher so I couldn't have any. But I got a piece of herring from a lady selling fish. It was the kind Mama called schmaltz herring. It was salty but I liked it.

Vanya bought a present for his mother. There were lots of people selling some things called verbos. They braid flowers and grasses into pretty designs and attach them to sticks. Vanya said his Mama would take it to church on the Sunday before Easter and then keep it at home after that.'

I found a place that was selling the heart shaped honey cookies. I bought one for Mama and one for Sarah with their names written on them in the Lithuanian writing.

Then we saw some gypsies leading some bears around in a circle. We got very excited because we knew they were Smorgon bears. The bears danced while a gypsy played a balalaika. One of the bears was pulling a small cart. As it came by the gypsy leading the bear said to us, "Get in the cart and I'll give you a ride." We both knew the voice. It was Avram. But we didn't act like we knew him because we knew he was wanted by the police.

We got in the cart and the bear pulled us around through the fair. "Follow us to see the famous Smorgon Bears dance and fight!" Avram called out in Lithuanian, Russian, Polish and Yiddish. But in between he talked quietly to us. We told him we came with our fathers so they could come to the trial. He had already seen Dvoira so he knew our fathers where dressed as wagon drivers.

"It's a good idea that they are dressed like drivers," he said. "There will be lots of drivers at the trial. It's something for them to do while they wait to drive their wagons back where they came from."

"What will happen to our sisters and the others at the trial?"

asked Vanya.

"They will be found guilty and sentenced to be sent to Siberia. The trial is just for show to scare people. Your sisters are very brave. They will use the trial to tell people that they must join the revolution."

"But we'll never see them again," I said, beginning to cry in spite of myself.

"We have a plan," said Avram. "Dvoira already knows the plan. We'll make sure your sisters are safe and never get to Siberia."

By this time the bear had pulled us back to where the Smorgon bagels were being sold. We got out of the wagon and thanked Avram for the ride. Dvoira saw us and came over to offer a bagel to the bear. She acted like she was afraid of the bear and Avram took the bagel from her and fed it to the bear who gobbled it down. While this happened a few quiet words passed between them. Then Avram led the bear away calling on people to follow him to see the dancing bears.

Vanya and I played for a while and then tried to think of what the plan might be. One thing we knew is that somehow we would be helping rescue our sisters.

When our fathers came back we told them we'd seen Avram. Dvoira came over to tell Papa and Father Vasily the first part of the plan. Most of the wagons would be leaving the next day, on Saturday. The Jewish drivers would wait until Sunday to drive back. But Father Vasily and Papa would not head back until Monday. They would take supplies like sacks of wheat and animal skins back to Smorgon. Dvoira said she would tell us the rest on the way back to Smorgon. I thought that Papa and Father Vasily would be upset but they looked pleased and didn't seem to be too surprised.

We ate a lunch of Jewish salami and black bread Mama had given Dvoira and some pirogi, cakes filled with potato, that Vanya's Mama had made.

Then we went back to the courthouse with our Papas. There was a large crowd in front, when we got there. I didn't see how we would be able to get into the courthouse, but Rabbi Eliezer's servant found us and took us up to the front door where the rabbi was waiting. I guessed he had already met Father Vasily because they nodded to each other. Rabbi Eliezer said something to the policeman at the door and he stepped out of our way to let us in.

The court room was very big. There were policemen standing around the sides and a lot of people were already sitting. Some people were sitting at tables in the front. We found some seats on one side. In a little while someone in uniform told us all to stand up and three men in robes came in and sat at a high table facing the room. Then we all sat down.

Pretty soon a door near the front of the courtroom opened and five prisoners were brought in. Anna and Dunya were there and three men I knew from Smorgon. I'd seen them wearing red armbands at the rally.

Anna looked slowly around the room and smiled just a little bit when she saw us but she didn't wave or show she knew us. Dunya did the same. Some of the people in the room started to clap their hands when the prisoners came in but one judge banged with a wooden hammer and told them to be quiet or they would have to leave.

Papa took a handkerchief from his pocket and wiped his eyes a little and squeezed my hand.

The trial itself was pretty boring. Different people were called up and told bad things about Anna and her friends.

"They passed out papers."

"They led the workers away from their jobs."

"They said bad things about the Governor and the Czar."

One man wore a mask over his head. Some people in the court booed when he came in and the judge told them to be quiet. The man in the mask said he had been a secret member of the movement and said the prisoners had been planning to kill the Governor and police chief in Smorgon.

People called out "Liar! Traitor!" in Yiddish, and the judge banged and shouted "Order! Order!"

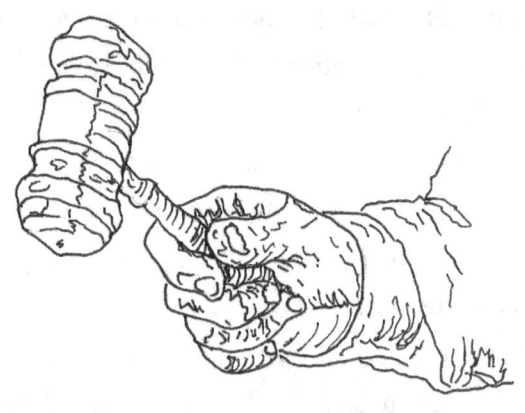

Then they got each prisoner to get up in the front and some men asked them questions. Did they do this? Did they do that? The questions were all in Russian. Two of the men kept answering, "I don't understand Russian" to each question. One of the judges told them they could sit down.

The third man made a short speech in Russian. I could only understand a little. He talked about the bad conditions of the leather workers and that the bosses and the Czar took everything from the workers and gave them nothing to help them. When Dunya came up she spoke in Belarussian and said about the same thing I guess. When she finished she raised her fist and shouted, "Svoboda!" which is freedom in Russian. The people in the court shouted back, "Svoboda!" When she finished I saw Father Vasily looked pale and I thought I saw a tear in his eye.

Then it was Anna's turn and she spoke in Yiddish.

"Speak Russian!" ordered the judge but she went on in Yiddish.

She told about how bad things were for everyone but how they were particularly bad for the Jews. They couldn't own land, they couldn't have certain jobs and they were always attacked by the Cossacks and the Czar's soldiers. At the end she shouted in Yiddish, "Down with Autocracy! Down with persecution of Jews and others! Long live the people's revolution!" The people in the court cheered even though the judge banged for order.

"She's doomed herself," I heard Papa say under his breath.

After that the three judges left the room. But they weren't gone long. The one who had been banging for order told the prisoners to stand and face him. He spoke in Russian but I knew what he was saying. They were guilty and on the following Monday they would be sent by train to Siberia. Dunya, Anna and the three men held their arms straight out in front them making a fist and they shouted together, "Long live the people's revolution!" over and over in all the languages they knew. Then they turned and walked out of the door that they came in with policemen walking in front and in back of them. As they got outside we could hear people cheering and shouting, "Long live the people's revolution!"

We went back to the fair and Papa and Father Vasily helped to load their wagons with the supplies that would go back to Smorgon. Our wagon had big sacks of wheat, salt and sugar.

Then we took the wagons to a barn at the edge of the fairgrounds where they would be kept until early Monday morning. Dvoira came with us to the Great Synagogue because it was Friday night. The other girls went to stay with Jewish families in Vilna and then went home on one of the other bagel wagons on Sunday.

Father Vasily and Vanya went to spend Saturday and Sunday with an orthodox priest in Vilna who was an old friend of their family. Father Vasily had promised to do the Sunday service there.

Saturday, Papa spent the whole day in the Great Synagogue. Dvoira slept late and I went with Papa to the synagogue in the morning. In the afternoon Dvoira and I walked around Vilna. Most of the signs on the stores on the streets around the synagogue were in Yiddish and the stores were closed for Shabbos.

Sunday, Papa borrowed a carriage and we went to the Jewish Cemetery to see the graves of our relatives buried there. I had a big shock. I got a few steps ahead of Papa and Dvoira and when I turned back to look for them there was a tombstone that said Duvid Mendel Gutman in Yiddish. I let out a gasp and Dvoira caught up with me to see what was wrong.

"That's your grandfather," she said. "The one you were named after."

You can imagine my dream that night! It was full of ghosts named Duvid Mendel.

Ten

Purim and the Rescue: March 1905

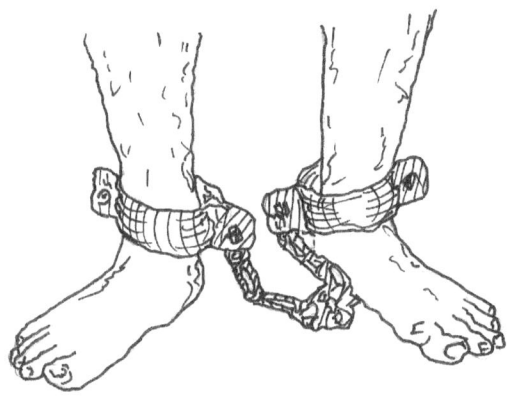

Early Monday morning while it was still dark, we met Father Vasily and Vanya at the Fairgrounds. Dvoira and I helped Papa hitch up the horses. Besides us, the only wagons that were left belonged to the gypsy caravan. The gypsies were busy getting ready to move out too.

I got excited when I saw that the wagon with the Smorgon bears was with the gypsy caravan. Vanya and I ran over to look for Avram. But he wasn't there. Dvoira came and told us Avram had something else to do and we would probably see him later.

She told Papa and Father Vasily part of the escape plan. We were supposed to stay with the gypsy caravan until we got to the woods near Ashmiany.

When the gypsy caravan moved out, we followed them. This time hardly any other wagons were on the road but us and the gypsies. Papa let me ride with Vanya and his Papa. There was nothing to see outside so we sat in the wagon on top of the smelly animal skins. We tried to think of what the plan was to save our sisters and the others. I thought maybe Avram was going to have bears attack the train. But Vanya reminded me that the soldiers on the train would have guns and would probably shoot the bears. He thought that the people from the movement might cut a tree down across the train tracks and stop the train. Then they would shoot the soldiers and save our sisters. But I said that the wrong people might get shot. We couldn't think of any plan that would work. So we wrestled for a while until Father Vasily said we were shaking the wagon and bothering the horses.

"Tag, you're it!" called Vanya. And he poked me and jumped out of the wagon and started running. I chased him. It was getting light out. Some gypsy boys and girls wanted to play too. We had fun until Papa called us to come back to his wagon.

"Why don't you practice your writing for a while?" he said.

I took a small slate I had brought with me and Vanya and I sat on the sacks of grain in our wagon. I wrote my name and his in Hebrew letters, and he wrote them in Russian letters. Then we wrote different things and tried to guess what the other one had written. Pretty soon we were thinking of insults. I wrote "Narishe bucher" in Yiddish (foolish boy). He wrote "Bolshoi durak" in Russian (big fool). That started us rolling around laughing and wrestling.

That's what we were doing when the caravan stopped in a place where the woods were thick on both sides of the road. The tree tops almost touched each other across the road so we could hardly see the sky. The gypsies began to get a meal ready and invited us to eat with them. Father Vasily and Vanya joined them but Papa politely said no, we had brought our own food. We still had some salami left and Papa had bought some delicious rolls in Vilna. They tasted as good as the Challah, the twisted egg bread, we ate on Shabbos. He also took his knife and cut an apple he got in Vilna for us to share. Dvoira and I were surprised that it tasted different from the apples that grew in Karka. This apple was sweet but we liked the sour Karka apples better.

Father Vasily and Vanya finished their lunch and came back to us.

"The next part of the plan is simple," said Dvoira. "We just wait here."

So we waited.

Vanya and I explored the area. The birch trees had no leaves yet. We gathered some pine cones to take home. There were patches of snow around and we saw some small animal tracks. Avram had taught me how to tell some of them and I thought I recognized rabbit and raccoon tracks.

A little ways away from where we stopped, we followed some fox tracks into another road leading away from our road. It was hardly more than a path, just wide enough for one wagon. Then we both stopped and looked at each other. Something was coming. We heard wagon wheels and also what sounded like several horses. We climbed a tree to see what was coming. For a minute we couldn't see anything and then we got a glimpse of a Russian soldier's uniform and behind him a wagon with a cover over it.

We climbed down fast and ran back to where our wagons were

waiting.

"Papa," I called, "there are soldiers and a wagon coming this way."

"What should we do, they'll be here in a few minutes?" Vanya said breathlessly.

"Just as they planned it," said Dvoira.

"They planned for soldiers?" Papa asked.

"If the plan worked, there will be soldiers," she answered.

Six soldiers turned into our road followed by a wagon. And surprise! The first soldier was Avram. He looked much different as a soldier than he had looked as a gypsy, but it was certainly Avram.

The gypsies seemed to recognize Avram too, because they began to laugh and surround him, pounding him on the back.

And out of the wagon jumped Anna and Dunya and their three comrades from the trial. Vanya and I ran to our sisters and they picked us up and hugged us. Then they hugged their Papas and Dvoira too.

"You're dressed like soldiers," said Vanya.

"What great costumes!" I said.

"They're not all costumes," said Avram.

"So the plan worked," Dvoira said. "You rescued them from the train."

"Without firing a shot and nobody knows yet," said Avram. "And all thanks to Captain Gutinsky here."

An older soldier with a fancier uniform than the others came up to Papa.

"Do you recognize me, Yankle Laib?" he said in Yiddish.

"God in heaven, it can't be you!" Papa gasped.

"Duvid Mendel, Dvoira, this is my cousin, Velvel, who I haven't seen for 25 years."

"I'm called Wolf now. Captain Wolf Gutinsky. The army made me take a Russian name."

"They took you away when you were 14 years old," said Papa. "The family gave you up for dead."

"And I almost died more than once," said Wolf. "But I learned to be a good soldier. I did what they wanted me to do and they made me an officer. And I kept asking to be assigned to this area."

"And now that I'm home, I get my chance to repay the Czar for all that he has done for me."

"So what was this plan that worked so well," said Father Vasily after he'd been introduced to Captain Gutinsky.

"It's the Captain's plan," said Avram. "He came to us and said he could save the prisoners after they were sentenced. He got us uniforms and made out papers releasing the prisoners to him. We were waiting when the train stopped in Ashmiany."

"Let me tell it," said Anna. "We were sitting in a separate car on the train, the five of us and six soldiers and a big mean woman, Ludmilla, who wouldn't even let us go to the toilet by ourselves. We had shackles on our hands and on our feet."

"She was much meaner than any of the soldiers," said Dunya.

Anna continued. "Then we saw that the train was slowing down and we could see we were coming into the Ashmiany station. We could see people from other railroad cars getting off and new passengers getting on. But then we saw this group of Russian soldiers waiting to get on our car. The officer in charge, who we now know was Captain Gutinsky, knocked on the window."

"New orders! he shouted. Open the door so we can come aboard! One of the soldiers guarding us unlocked the door to let them in."

Anna went on with her story.

"I have this order to release your prisoners to us, said the Captain. It's signed by General Karpovich."

"Why would the General want us to release the prisoners to you? asked our guard."

"We have word that an attempt is going to be made to free these prisoners, said the Captain. I head a unit specially trained to deal with attempted escapes. We'll take your prisoners on a different train with a different route so their comrades won't know where they are."

"Our guard took the paper from Captain Gutinsky. He looked it over carefully. Here's the General's personal seal. Everything seems to be in order, he said."

"The General wants you to stay on the train until Minsk, said Captain Gutinsky. Then you are to return to your unit in Vilnius. Tell them only that by order of the General you were relieved of your prisoners."

"The guards cheered. We don't have to take them all the way to Siberia. Hurrah!"

"What about me? said Ludmilla I suppose you'll need me to guard the women."

"These are dangerous revolutionaries, women or not, said Captain Gutinsky. They don't deserve special treatment. We'll do the guarding ourselves."

"Dunya and I were really scared," said Anna. "We didn't know what would happen to us."

"Captain Gutinsky and his special unit got us roughly on our feet. We'll need the keys to these shackles, he said. Our guard handed them to him. Then he unlocked our leg shackles so we could walk off the train ourselves. The soldiers walked in front of and behind us while Captain Gutinsky walked alongside and shouted at us to stay close together and move fast. At the end of the platform there was a wagon waiting with a soldier sitting on the driver's seat."

Dunya cut in. "That was the first time we knew we were being rescued. The soldier was Avram."

Anna went on. "Don't do or say anything and keep looking scared, said Captain Gutinsky softly. They forced us to get into the wagon and then mounted their horses and we rode off with Avram driving the wagon and the soldiers in front and in back of us."

"Only when we were safely away from the station and coming into the forest did Captain Gutinsky order a halt. Then they took off our shackles and Avram introduced Captain Gutinsky and told us how he had come to leaders of the Movement and offered this plan for rescuing us from the train to Siberia," Anna finished.

"We were freed without a shot being fired," Dunya said. "All thanks to the mysterious Captain Gutinsky."

"We were ready to fight if they wouldn't let them go with us," said the Captain. "But they actually cheered when we told them they could go back to Vilna and didn't have to take the prisoners all the way to Siberia."

"But, Velvel, won't they find out what happened and that you were involved?" said Papa.

"Actually, I signed the commanding general's name and used his seal on the papers," said Wolf.

"Eventually they'll figure out what happened and maybe even that it was me, but I won't be using this uniform very much longer."

"So what's the next part of the plan, Cousin Velvel?" I said.

"It's been a long time since anyone called me that, young man," he said. "But for now it might be best to call me 'Captain'. These young men are going to change to gypsy clothes. Dunya and Anna will wear some peasant dresses and ride with their Papas. And my 'soldiers' and I will be your escort in case anyone stops you on the way home. The commanding general is away in St. Petersburg for the rest of this month so it's not likely anyone will realize there's anything wrong for quite a while. Avram will change from soldier to gypsy clothes again so anybody looking for him would not recognize him."

"It's almost Purim and everybody's wearing costumes," I said. Everybody laughed.

On the way back to Smorgon Papa told my sisters and me how his cousin had become a soldier. The Czar made young boys go into the army. People with money could pay to keep their sons from going or pay someone to take their place. "Velvel's Papa had died and the family didn't have the money to buy him out," Papa said sadly. "So they took him away when he was only 14 years old. It was very hard for Jewish boys. They made them take Russian names and they couldn't get the right food."

"Poor cousin Velvel," I said.

"Not so long ago the Czar's soldiers used to take little Jewish boys as young as you," said Anna. "They took the oldest boy in each family. A lot of them died and those that lived forgot their families and where they came from."

Just before we came to Smorgon we stopped again in some woods. "Why are we stopping here?" I asked.

"It's time to say goodbye," said Anna giving me a hug. "Dunya,

Avram and I will stay with the gypsies until we get to a place where the Movement will hide us."

"And these men and I will make a camp in the woods so that we can fight against the Czar," said Captain Gutinsky.

"But after 25 years the family will want to see you," said Papa.

"It would be too dangerous for you and for me if anyone finds out I am here," he said. "I intend to stay not far from here. There are woods and caves for us to hide in. Sometime soon you'll see me again, my dear cousin."

Cousin Velvel lifted me up and said, "You understand, clever boy, you must not tell anyone outside of your family you saw me or how your sister escaped."

Another secret I had to keep. I promised not to tell anyone. So did Vanya. "Can we come and see your camp?" said Vanya.

"Absolutely not," said Father Vasily. "You must forget that there even is a camp somewhere in these woods."

"And how will we know how you are?" Father Vasily said to Dunya.

 "For now we have to stay in hiding. We'll get word to Dvoira at the bagel bakery," said Dunya. "Anna and Avram and I will take care of each other."

After more hugs and kisses they were gone. Papa and Father Vasily drove their wagons on the road to Smorgon and Vanya and I walked alongside the wagons. We didn't feel like playing anymore.

"I'm glad they escaped," I said.

"Me too," said Vanya.

We were quiet for a few minutes.

"They'll be OK," I said.

"Sure they can take care of themselves," Vanya said.

And then we didn't talk for a long time. I was trying to keep from crying and I think so was Vanya.

Pretty soon we started passing farms near Smorgon and then we were in the town. "I have to leave you now, Yankle Laib," Father Vasily called to Papa.

"Thank you for coming to Vilna with us, Vasily Ivanovitch," Papa replied. "We'll all pray that our brave but foolish daughters are safe."

"God be with them and with you too, my friend," said Father Vasily.

"Amen," said Papa.

Vanya and I looked at each other. He stuck his hand out and I shook it. Then he climbed up on the wagon with his Papa and they turned into the leather maker's street and we went on to the street of the bagel bakeries. Dvoira had to stay there to help unpack the grain and give her boss the money from the fair. She would come home on Friday night as usual.

Sarah came running to meet us when we came walking down the street in Karka to our house. Mama was standing in the door. Sarah hugged Papa and me.

"Tell us all about your trip and the trial," Sarah burst out.

Mama gave me a hug and then she kissed Papa like I'd never seen them kiss before.

"But what about the trial?" said Sarah.

"Bad news and good news," said Papa. "The bad news is they were found guilty and sent to Siberia. The good news is they escaped from the train near Ashmiany. We left them just outside Smorgon. They'll be hiding near here for a while."

For an instant Mama turned pale and her knees buckled. I

thought she was going to fall, but she steadied herself and said quietly, "Oh, thank God."

"I want to hear the whole story," said Sarah.

"Just thank God they're home and Anna is safe," said Mama. "That's enough for now. There will be time later for the whole story."

"So now get out of those ridiculous clothes," she said.

"Papa and Rabbi Eliezer played a good trick on the other rabbis at the Great Synagogue," I said.

And I told them the whole story including how Papa had me read from the Torah and how wise everyone thought he was.

I would have told them more but Mama said, "You're a clever boy and a dirty, smelly one. I'll heat some water for a bath for you both."

I never liked Mama giving me a bath particularly when she combed my hair with a fine tooth comb as she always did to make sure I didn't have any lice. But I didn't mind that at all this time. It felt really good to soak in a nice warm tub.

At dinner time I gave Mama and Sarah the heart-shaped cookies from the fair with their names written on them. Papa showed them the things he bought for our Shalach Monis plate. And they heard the whole story of how Cousin Velvel, who was now Captain Gutinsky, had rescued Anna and Dunya from the train with his clever plan. Mama couldn't believe Cousin Velvel was still alive.

It was so good to sleep in my place on the stove in the kitchen that night.

We didn't know when we would see Anna again. I felt good that she had escaped, but I had to act sad because everybody in Karka and Smorgon had heard that she and the others were found guilty at the trial and sent to Siberia. No one knew about the escape. It wasn't hard to act sad because I really missed Anna. We had so little time together on the way back to Smorgon. As it turned out it was not so long before I saw her again and when I did it was a big surprise.

What a Purim we had in 1905! Purim is always a lot of fun because we have costume parades and we get to eat and drink and gamble. Kids have noise makers called grogers. You swing them around in a circle and they make a loud noise.

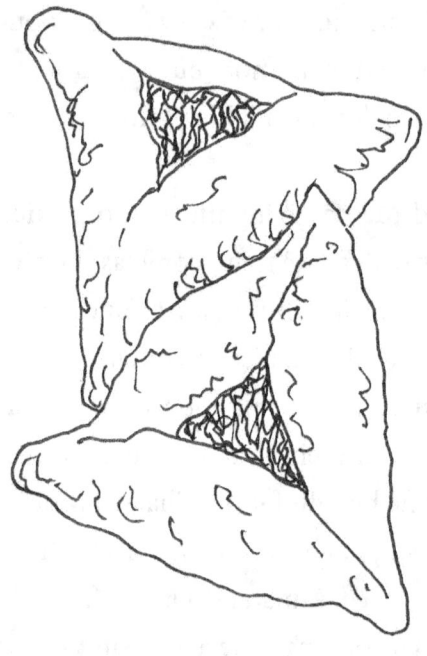

Mama bakes some three cornered cakes called hamantashen. That's because Haman, the Purim villain, wore a hat that had three corners. She puts prunes or cherries or little black poppy seeds in the middle of her hamantashen.

This year it seemed like Purim had already started for us even though it was still two weeks off. Papa and Father Vasily and Avram were wearing costumes at the fair in Karka. And as it turned out we saw more costumes before we got back to Smorgon.

Since Kate and Maish were married, Maish's family, the Krupnicks, were now part of our family.

Among Jews, people related to you by marriage are family, machatunim. Papa invited them to come to our little shul in Karka to hear him read the Megillah, the story of Queen Esther. It takes a very long time to read the whole Megillah. We all listened politely and whenever Haman was mentioned in the story the kids all made noise with the grogers.

And then the Krupnicks invited us to their house for a Purim party. Sarah and I were really excited when we found out that Maish's father had hired a group of performers to do a Purim Shpiel. The Krupnicks lived in a big house right on the central square in Smorgon. The house had a second floor with a stairway leading up to it. Sarah and I went up to the second floor with Maish's sisters and brothers. We looked out the bedroom windows. You could see the square and a lot of the town.

Mama brought some of her homemade hamantashen. And there were lots of different kinds of good things to eat. I especially liked a kind of candy called halvah made from sesame seeds. It melts in your mouth.

Everybody dressed up in costumes. A lot of the girls were dressed like Queen Esther or Vashti who was the Queen before Esther. The king sent her away because she wouldn't dance in front of his banquet guests. The boys were dressed as Esther's Uncle Mordechai or the King or the villain Haman with his three-cornered hat. The grown-ups were dressed like peasants, gypsies, animals, soldiers. Papa wore his wagon driver outfit. I guess it reminded him of his adventure.

The klezmers played a march and we all walked around in a big circle to show our costumes.

Then I saw Maish's father motion to the klezmers' leader and they began to play a lively dance tune. And from the back of the house came the Purim Shpielers all in costumes and all wearing masks. They danced as they came to the front of the very large room where we all were sitting.

We thought that under their costumes the players were Yeshiva students. Usually they even played the parts of the women in the play.

The play started with someone dressed as a Rabbi reading a very long scroll in a deep voice that disappeared into a mumble. The rabbi mumbled on and pretty soon all the other players had fallen asleep and were loudly snoring. Then some of the characters seemed to wake up from their sleep. Three characters came forward and did the Russian Dance called the Kazatska going down to the floor on each step. They were the King, Haman, and a wise man. All were dressed like Russians but Haman had a three-corner hat. The King looked a lot like the Czar. The three men were arguing. Haman kept calling out, "Send them to Siberia!" The Czar/King kept saying, "My people all love to work and slave for me." The third man was Mordechai who kept stroking this long beard.

After that there were songs and dances and little funny parts of the story of Queen Esther. But somehow everything seemed to come back to the villains of our time - the Czar, the Cossacks, the

Czarina (the Czar's wife), the Governor. I watched Maish's father when one of players was dressed like the rich boss of a leather factory and sat in the corner counting gold rubles and mumbling, "My beautiful gold rubles." Maish's father laughed as hard as anyone. Then a player dressed like a bear came out but the bear had a dress and a crown on and the other players bowed down to the bear and called her Queen Esther and then they sang a song to the bear about how beautiful she was.

Just as the pretend rabbi was finally reaching the end of his very long Megillah scroll, there was a noise from the back of the house and three Russian soldiers wearing masks rushed in. They pointed guns at all the players and told them they were under arrest and they would be sent to Siberia for being bad actors. One of them shot a gun and a flag came out that said, "Happy Purim."

We all clapped and made noise with our grogers.

And then the players took off their masks and everybody gasped. There were Anna, Dunya and Avram in the soldier's uniforms. Some of the other players were their friends from the movement who had been arrested with them. And the bear was Captain Gutinsky. Maish's father thanked them all for the fine Purim Shpiel.

After the play there was more good food. I saw Papa and Mama go upstairs with Captain Gutinsky. When they came down Mama was crying and I heard her say, "Our Anna was saved by a miracle."

"Thank God," said Papa.

"God and Cousin Velvel," I thought to myself. But I didn't say anything.

After everyone but our two families had left Maish's father said to Anna, "Why did you send word to me that you wanted to have the Purim Shpiel at my house. Wasn't it risky to come out of your hiding to show yourselves here?"

"We thought with all the costumes and masks it was a perfect way to see our friends and families," said Anna. "But there was another reason. Avram, Dunya and I have to leave here. Our friends in the movement think it is too dangerous for us to stay. By now the Czar's police will figure out we never got to Siberia. After the big public trial it will look ridiculous that we escaped so they will really be after us. We're going to America. We'll be with Kate and Maish in Chicago We're leaving right away. We had to take the chance to see you before we go. Right now Avram and Dunya have gone to say goodbye to their families."

More good news and bad news. The good news was that we had a really happy Purim. The bad news was that it ended with everybody crying because we were losing Anna again.

Eleven
Passover 1906 When I Was Nine

So it was just after Purim in 1905 that Anna left us to join Kate in Chicago. It was hard for Mama and Papa to see her go. Mama was sure she would never see her again. Papa said, "We've lost her twice. Once when she deserted our way of life for her 'movement' and now when she goes half way around the world and deserts her family."

Anna started to cry. "I've never left you, Papa. I'll always be proud of you and Mama and my family. I'll always be proud of being

Jewish. But I have to fight for the rights of Jews and everyone else to live free lives. I promise I'll work in Chicago and send money like Kate does to bring our whole family there. I promise we'll be together again soon."

In the end Anna went off the way Kate had gone with all our tears and Papa's blessing.

It didn't go so easily for Dunya and Avram. I was only a kid but I saw the way they were always together and the way they looked at each other. So it was no surprise when Anna asked Papa if he would marry them before they left.

I expected Papa to be upset. But he shook his head sadly and quietly said, "No, it cannot be. First of all I don't believe anything good can come from such a marriage between a Jew and a Christian. Can a fish marry a chicken? They are different. What kind of life would they have together? And second, if I, a rabbi, married them the marriage would not be considered legal anyway."

"But in America–" said Anna.

Papa cut her off. "So maybe in America a fish can marry a chicken. Let them be married in America, then."

It was Dunya's father who was most angry. Vanya told me that when Dunya told him she and Avram were leaving for America and wanted to be married, he stamped his foot and said, "Jews are Jews and Christians are Christians. What kind of a priest would I be if I let my daughter marry a Jew? Avram is a strange fellow who keeps the company of bears. Better he should marry a bear than my daughter."

"He's kind and gentle and we love each other, Papa," said Dunya. That didn't help.

"Never, never will I allow this!" he shouted. Dunya's mother cried but she didn't do anything to change Father Vasily's mind.

In the end Dunya and Avram went off without being married. Anna wrote us later that the captain of the ship married them on the way across the Atlantic. After that it seemed like Father Vasily blamed Papa for what happened. He never came to visit Papa and I never got to play with Vanya.

That is until Passover in 1906 when I was nine.

One thing my father and my sisters agree about is that Passover started when Jews got out of slavery a long time ago in Egypt. Every year we celebrate how Moses led the Jews out of slavery and into the promised land. But the story isn't the same for all of them. Papa says Moses was sent by God to lead the Jews out of slavery. My sisters say he and his brother Aaron and sister Miriam were revolutionary leaders who organized their people to free themselves from the Egyptian Pharaoh, just as they and their friends in the movement are organizing the people to rise up against the Czar.

Papa says God sent plagues to convince Pharaoh to let our people go. Anna says the only plagues that the working people of Russia can threaten the Czar with are strikes and revolution. Papa says the Torah says to teach your children we were once slaves in Egypt so they will be grateful for the lives they now have. Kate says we teach them we were slaves who freed ourselves so they may understand that today also they can free themselves from the bosses and the Czar.

Eight nights and days we celebrated Passover with this argument. That is until Kate and Anna were gone. Dvoira tried to get the argument started but Papa gave her one of his evil eye looks and she stopped. I've got my own idea. Passover is the time when Papa is busy supervising the making of matzo, Mama and my sisters go crazy cleaning the house, and people who can afford them get new clothes. And poor kids like me get somebody's old clothes.

Most families in Karka and Smorgon have a lot of kids. In most families if I was the youngest boy I'd get clothes passed down to me by older brothers but I have only older sisters. We have a system in Smorgon. It's called "taking care of our own." Jews don't depend on outsiders to help us. So people who have money give some of it to take care of our old people, to provide wood for poor people in the winter, to provide an egg bread or a chicken for Friday night for those that can't afford their own, to provide weddings for poor girls and to bury people who die too poor to afford a funeral. And they collect clothes and give them to children whose parents are poor.

So that's how I get my clothes. They're really old clothes. Probably several boys in a family wore them before they got to me. They look worn and Mama has to patch the knees and sew on buttons and make them shorter or longer or tighten them or loosen them. Some of my pants have an extra piece of cloth that doesn't match on the bottom of the legs that Mama added to make them long enough for me. Some of my shirts have sleeves that don't match. I don't mind too much. Most kids in Karka wear old patched clothes like mine.

I shouldn't really complain. But just once I was hoping to go to the market or to the tailor and get some new clothes that I would be the first one to wear. You know by now that I'm always looking for ways to make money. I got this idea that I could figure out a lot of ways of making some money to buy my own clothes. In the woods there are nuts, and berries and mushrooms at different times of the year. I could gather them and sell them and make money like I did when I was younger. Some of the best mushrooms grow in the woods in springtime even though it's still pretty cold around where we lived. Maish and Kate took me with them once to pick mushrooms in the woods in the early spring and I was pretty sure I could find that place again. You have to be careful about picking mushrooms because some of them are poison. I decided if I only picked one kind I knew were good I'd be safe about that.

The problem was there was a lot of stuff going on at home for me to do in the days before Passover. Our house isn't very big. It has a main room with the stove in the middle. There's a little room off the main room that's full of benches where Papa teaches me and the other boys. That room has its own door so the boys can come and go without coming into the rest of the house. I sleep on top of the stove in the main room. Sarah used to sleep there too, but when Anna left she moved to the very small room the girls share that Papa and some neighbors built on the back of the house. Sarah has it to herself now except when Dvoira is home. There's also a kitchen with a fireplace. The whole house had to be cleaned and washed and swept for Passover. Sarah was busy helping Mama. There were no bagels baked during Passover so Dvoira would be home the whole eight days to help Mama.

Since Anna left, Papa was giving me special lessons with a few of the older boys who were getting ready to go to the Yeshiva. These lessons took up almost all my time. It seemed like he was in a hurry to teach me everything that most boys didn't learn until they were 13 and had their Bar Mitzvah. I didn't mind too much. It gave me a lot more time with Papa and I kind of enjoyed talking with him about the Torah and Talmud. He really was smart when it came to those things. I already was at the point where I could have done most of the Passover Seder myself and I was only nine years old.

But at Passover, Papa was too busy to give me the extra lessons.

Passover was Papa's busiest time because he supervised the matzah baking for most of Smorgon. When Moses led the Jews out of Egypt they couldn't stop to make bread. Usually something is put in bread to make air bubbles and make it rise. But that takes time. So the Jews running away from Egypt just mixed the dough, rolled it out flat and baked it into round or square pieces that were crisp and flat. So for all eight days of Passover we eat this flat crisp bread called matzah. And we don't eat any other bread or cake or anything that rises.

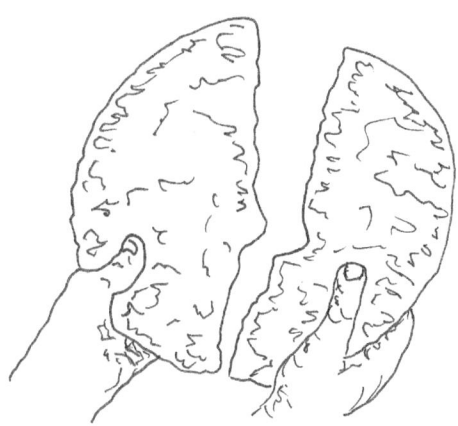

But Mama can use the matzah to make all kinds of wonderful things. She breaks it up into small pieces and mixes it with eggs and fries it in butter. She calls that matzah brei. Sometimes Mama makes a pudding, a kugel, from matzah and eggs and apples and raisins. Or she just breaks it up into small pieces we call farfel and we put that in our soup.

If Mama grinds up the matzah into a fine powder, we call that matzah meal. She can make pancakes with that or cakes or cookies. But my favorite is the balls she makes of matzah meal and fresh eggs she calls kneidlach, matzah balls. She boils them in salted water and they come out perfectly round and fluffy and we eat them in our chicken soup. I asked Papa once how come if we eat matzah because the Jews had to suffer when they ran away from slavery, then why can we make so many good things to eat from the matzah? Papa says that shows that poor people can turn any simple food into a feast if they are content with what they have. And if you have a cook who knows a few tricks, Mama says.

Karka has a flour mill. Our little house is between the mill and the Karka Shul. Our neighbors bring their rye and wheat to be ground into flour in the mill. Papa didn't make the matzah but it was his job to make sure it was made right. And at Passover special flour was prepared at the mill. Papa's work started in the fall before Passover when the wheat was harvested. He had to go to the fields to make sure it was done properly. Only two of our neighbors could grow this special wheat in special fields. Then it had to be brought to a special warehouse where Papa looked at it to make sure no water could get in to start the wheat to grow or spoil. Just before Passover, the wheat was brought to the mill where Papa and the Smorgon rabbis met the wagons and supervised unloading and storing it. If any was spoiled or sprouting they burned it up and got rid of it.

Finally, when it was time to bake the Passover Matzah, the wheat was ground on a special mill stone and mixed with water which could only come from our specially blessed well. The squares of matzah were rolled out and boys from the Yeshiva in Smorgon used a wheel to make slits in the matzah that made it crisp.

I was kept busy by both Papa and Mama running errands and doing extra chores. For Mama, I had to bring water from the well, get eggs from a neighbor, check every corner of the house to make sure there were no bread crumbs. And I had to catch the chicken our neighbors had sent over for Papa to kill for our Passover dinner. For Papa, I had to carry messages to the other rabbis and bring him samples of the matzah to check as they came out of the ovens. I was really kept busy like everyone else in our family. But that gave me an idea. If I just slipped off into the woods without telling anybody and without anybody seeing me, Mama would think I was helping Papa and Papa would think I was helping Mama and I would have time to go and pick my mushrooms. It seemed like a great idea at the time.

So after I delivered a message for Papa I just slipped into the edge of the woods making sure no one saw me. The woods come right down to the edge of the beautiful little lake just behind our house. I was in the woods just passing the lake shore when I saw a large group of people coming toward me following Father Vasily. At first I was scared. I thought they were coming to Karka to make trouble for us Jews, but then I saw they were going to the lake.

Passover is a Spring holiday but it doesn't really get warm in Smorgon until late June and the lake stays frozen until the middle of April. I hid at the edge of the woods and watched. They all stopped and Father Vasily said some words in a language I didn't understand. Then some men went out on the ice and began cutting the ice with axes and saws. They took a rope that was tied to a cart pulled by three horses. We call that kind of cart a troika. They tied the other end around the ice and pulled it out of the lake. When they got it out they chipped the ice with their axes until it was in the shape of a big, heavy cross.

I wasn't sure but I guessed this had something to do with Easter, the holiday they have at the same time as Passover. I knew they painted eggs with beautiful designs. And I knew that this was a dangerous time for Jews because Easter was about Christ dying and some Christians said that in old times Jews killed Christ. Maish told me that Christ was a Jew who made trouble for the Romans. So they killed him by nailing him to a cross. I guess that's why the people were making this ice cross. They tied this big heavy ice cross to the priest's back and he began to lead them back toward Smorgon. Father Vasily is big but I couldn't believe how strong he was to carry such a heavy cross. As the people worked they sang beautiful songs and when they left they sang a song that sounded familiar - like maybe I heard it in another year.

As I started off in the woods, there right in front of me was Vanya. I'd hardly seen him since Purim the year before. His Papa never came to talk to Papa anymore. Vanya was sucking on a piece of ice chipped from the cross and he held out a piece for me. I felt good that he was sharing with me. He was dressed in old patched clothes like I was, not much different than mine. I told him that I was going to pick mushrooms so I could sell them and get new clothes for myself. Vanya decided to come along to pick mushrooms too. He was bored with all the Easter activities at his house and right away he wanted to go with me.

I said, "Shouldn't you ask your father if you can go?"

He laughed and said, "And did you ask your father? We'll be back before they even know we were gone. Besides he doesn't seem to like me playing with you since Dunya left."

I was glad for the company. I'd missed Vanya. We had a lot of fun on the way. I knew the woods pretty well but it was nice to have a friend with me. Mostly our woods have white birch trees and pines. The pines are green all year round and drop pine cones on the ground. In a few weeks the birch trees would get new leaves and tiny strawberries would grow under them. On the branches of bushes there would be black or red currents. But now the branches were bare. Vanya showed me how to peel the white birch bark from the trees and make a kind of hat.

We pretended we were on a bear hunt and I showed Vanya what Avram had taught me about seeing where the bears had been and how fresh their tracks were. Then he pretended he was a bear and chased me and I climbed a tree and he came up after me. I pretended I was the bear trainer and made him dance. At one place we took turns throwing snowballs at a big wide tree. We had so much fun we lost track of time. And we got a little lost on the way to the place where I thought we'd find the mushrooms. Then I remembered to look for the tallest pine tree and we found the place. But it took us longer to get there than I thought it would.

When we got there we had to hunt for a while for the mushrooms. This kind of mushroom is very special, Maish told me. And they are the first mushrooms that come up in the Spring. They were growing right out of the snow. But we had to push some of the snow aside to get at them. We filled the sack I had brought with mushrooms. We both filled our hats with mushrooms and stuffed as many as we could in our shirts and our pants pockets. We teased each other about how fat we both looked stuffed with mushrooms.

On the way back we hurried because we didn't want to be

caught in the woods after dark. But we still played on the way and stopped now and then to look for tracks of bears and other animals. There were a few early flowers sticking up through the snow and we picked some for our mothers. We were running and playing tag all the way home and laughing as we came to the edge of the woods near my house.

We stopped to catch our breath just before we came out of the woods. It was then we heard the noise - a lot of noise. It sounded like angry people shouting. We could see a lot of people led by Vanya's father, the priest, but this time they were going right to the mill and not the lake.

"Why are they making so much noise?" said Vanya.

"They're going to the mill," I said. "Maybe there was an accident."

"But why is everybody so angry?" said Vanya.

At first we couldn't make out what anybody was shouting but as we got closer we could see the crowd of people had stopped in front of the mill and in the middle was Father Vasily. And on the steps and in the mill were Papa and the mill workers and the students who were there to make the matzah. It looked like the crowd around the priest was going to attack the Jews. Some were carrying farm tools like shovels and the sickles they used to cut wheat. The Jews were holding sticks and pieces of broken stones. Some of the Jewish farmers came running carrying their farm tools.

We heard someone shout, "Kill the Jews!" They grabbed the boy to use his blood to make their matzah when we came to the lake for the cross of ice!"

"They grabbed a boy?" said Vanya. "You use a kid's blood to make matzah?"

"Of course not," I said. "It couldn't happen. Blood is traif, forbidden. If a drop of blood fell on matzah Papa would make them get rid of the whole batch."

We didn't know what to do.

Now I heard Papa yelling, "You know me, Vasily Ivanovitch. You're a scholar like me. You know Jews don't kill Christian children."

Father Vasily looked angry and troubled.

"Don't listen to him, Father Vasily," said a big farmer holding a shovel.

Papa said, "Why would I harm your boy? My little boy is missing too. Maybe they've both been kidnapped? We should look for them together. We're wasting valuable time."

"Break down the door!" called someone else. "I bet we'll find Vanya's body inside!" The shouts got louder and the crowd pushed closer to Papa and the Jews in the mill.

Vanya and I looked at each other.

"They think we've been kidnapped," I said.

"They think I'm dead," said Vanya.

"We have to do something," I said.

And then a smile came on Vanya's face and he started singing loudly the beautiful Easter song I heard the procession singing. And I joined in, saying "bitty bum" when I couldn't pick up the words. The people stopped shouting and everyone turned to look at us. We put our arms around each other's shoulders and walked through the angry crowd, trying to look calm, until we stood between our fathers.

"We went into the woods to pick mushrooms," I said.

"And we found a lot," said Vanya showing his hat full of mushrooms.

Papa and Vanya's father looked very angry. But before they could do or say anything there were our two mothers picking us up and hugging us and smothering us with kisses. "Foolish boys," Mama said. "You gave us such a scare!"

Vanya's mother gave him a light slap on his bottom, but there were tears in her eyes as she held him tight. I got a potch on my tusch too - and not so light - but I didn't mind. I knew by her face how worried I had made Mama.

That night Papa and Mama and Sarah ate their supper while I was made to sit in the back of the house by myself. I was pretty sure I wouldn't get anything to eat that night. Finally Papa called me to come to him. His face was very strange looking.

Very quietly, Papa said, "Duvidka, you went into the woods to pick mushrooms?"

"Yes Papa," I said.

"And you went with Father Vasily's son. What's his name, Ivan?"

"Yes Papa. Vanya, he's my friend."

"Hmm. Friend. And neither of you asked your Papas if you could go or told anyone you were going?"

"No, Papa, we didn't tell anybody. We only wanted to get some mushrooms for our families for a surprise."

"You mean to sell and make money," said Papa.

"Yes Papa. I wanted to save some money to get a new shirt and new pants. But I always give Mama half the money."

"Now, Duvid Mendel, do you know what was happening when you came home?"

"Yes Papa," I said. "The Christians thought that Vanya had been kidnapped. But I don't understand about the blood."

"There are many lies told about what we Jews do," said Papa. "One of the most terrible lies is that we use the blood of Christian children to make our Passover matzah. Just a few years ago a Christian child got lost about this time of year in a town near here. And before he was found many Jews had been killed."

Papa's voice became even more quiet - I almost liked it better when he shouted at me.

"You and Vanya are children," he said. "Only nine years old. And children sometimes do foolish things without thinking about what might happen. Today you did a very bad thing. You frightened your families and your neighbors when we couldn't find you. And you almost caused a terrible, terrible thing to happen."

"But Papa," I said "We didn't mean to hurt anybody. We had fun in the woods. We played and we got a little lost." I started to cry. I couldn't help it.

Mama had been listening the whole time. "You're a little boy, Duvidka. It's not your fault that people believe bad things about each other," Mama said. "But now you understand why you can't just go off with a friend and not tell anyone. I've told you this is a dangerous time of year for us."

"Now you see why we keep to ourselves," said Papa "If we keep to ourselves and don't bother the gentiles they usually don't bother us," said Papa.

Just then Dvoira arrived from her job to spend the Passover week with us. I got to eat with Dvoira and Papa and Mama stopped giving each other worried looks. Mama had made a delicious soup of some of the mushrooms I had picked and a beef bone. Sarah told Dvoira the whole story as soon as she came in the door. But the story of what happened in Karka had already reached the bakery in Smorgon before Dvoira started for home.

"Our kliegele was not so smart today," said Dvoira. "The Czar and the bosses stir up the gentiles against the Jews so we won't see that we have a common enemy. They want us to fight each other instead of them."

"Eat your soup," said Mama, trying to head off another argument.

"This mushroom soup does taste good," said Dvoira. "But Duvid had better sell his mushrooms to our neighbors and not go into the market this year. It could be dangerous."

The next night just as I was about to get dressed for our Seder, the dinner we have for the first night of Passover, I found a package hanging on the gate with my name on it.

"Look Mama, look Papa," I said. "Someone left a package with my name written on it in Russian."

"Nu," said Mama. "So open it already."

In the package were a new pair of pants and a new shirt. I put them on and it was wonderful even if they were big for me. My first new clothes.

"It's all right," said Mama. "You'll grow into them."

"But who could have brought these clothes for me?" I said.

"Not me," said Dvoira "I give all my pay to Mama to save for our trip to America."

"Not Mama or me," said Papa. "We've been too busy and we don't have money for new clothes for any of us."

"Maybe the Prophet Elijah," said Mama. There were stories Jews told of how the Prophet Elijah did wonderful things for poor people at Passover time. We always put an extra glass of wine in the middle of our table for him. And during the Seder we opened the door for him to come in.

"Do you think it was Elijah, Papa?" I asked.

"Or perhaps somebody equally holy," said Papa.

At the Seder that night it was my job, as the youngest, to ask the four questions that are part of the Haggadah, the Passover story we read at each Seder. When I read the first question in Hebrew, "Why is this night different than all other nights?" it had a new answer for me. And when we sang the song in Hebrew to honor the profit Elijah, I sang it louder than anyone as I wondered about my new clothes:

Eliahu Hanovi
Eliahu Hatishbi
Eliahu, Eliahu
Eliahu, Ha Gilodi

I was sure that year that some of the wine from Elijah's cup disappeared during the Seder. And I wondered whether Elijah would be able to find us in America.

Twelve

Goodbye Karka, Goodbye Smorgon: April 1906

What happened at Passover with Vanya and me was pretty scary. I had nightmares. In one of them the lake was red with blood and Jews and Christians were fighting in the blood/lake and Vanya and I were crying and standing on the shore shouting, "Stop! Stop! Don't you see we're alive?"

After Passover, Papa and Mama seemed to change somehow. Papa spent more of his time studying the Torah by himself. His lessons to the other boys seemed a bit strange like he had too much else on his mind. And after every lesson to me he would ask me to tell him how I was to live my life and what I must know. I even felt a little sorry for Sarah and Dvoira because he hardly paid attention to them at all.

Mama could talk about nothing except being with Kate and Anna in America. They'd been sending money regularly but it still wasn't nearly enough for tickets for all of us to leave. For her, after that Passover, there was no home for us in Karka or Smorgon. Papa had stopped arguing about leaving and only shook his head and said, "What will I do there? Ich vais nit. I don't know."

We all tried to tell him that people would still respect and honor him in America but he just shook his head. "In America, the little boys will go to public school. Who will come to a rebbe then?"

More of our neighbors were giving up farming because they couldn't make enough money to support their families. They were taking jobs in Smorgon or even moving to Vilna or Minsk. A few were leaving for America.

There were rumors of a former Russian officer, some even said a Jew, who had a large rebel group in the forest that was attacking army posts and government buildings. They called him "The Wolf." There was a story that he had attacked an army convoy and captured the payroll for the soldiers in Vilna. Another story was that poor families had found boxes of food on their door steps. One day I went to help Mama with her milk and we found a cage with six chickens in our yard. On the cage was a piece of paper with the Yiddish word Freiheit, freedom, written on it. Above the word was a picture of a wolf.

There were strikes and when the police were sent to arrest the strikers they were ambushed as they passed through the woods. There were even stories that the Cossacks were refusing orders to go into the woods to find the rebels because rebels set up traps to cripple their horses as they rode between the trees.

The Governor spread the story that the rebels were led by Jews and that the Jews were killing Christians. A mob attacked Jews in Kovno as they were coming out of the synagogue.

One Friday night, Dvoira came bursting into our house waving a letter and shouting, "Good news! Kate's going to have a baby!" The letter said that the baby would be born during the summer. Sarah and I danced around the room when we heard Dvoira.

Now you would have thought that would have made Mama and Papa happy too. But Mama burst into tears. "My first grandchild and I won't be there to see it," she sobbed.

"If it is a boy, how will we know if it is even circumcised?" said Papa.

Dvoira also brought an invitation from Maish's father inviting us to dinner on the next Friday night at his house. Papa didn't want to go but Mama said they were family and we couldn't refuse.

The Krupnick's house had a separate room with a table big enough for all of us to sit and eat. On the table was a beautiful linen table cloth. There were fancy dishes, real silver knives and forks and spoons and sparkling glasses with stems. Two beautiful gold candle sticks were on the table with a huge twisted Chalah, an egg bread, between them. Two servants were there to serve the meal.

Maish's father was very friendly. He asked Mama if she would light the Shabbos candles and say the blessing over them before dinner. Then he asked me and his son Shmuel to say the blessing over the bread. We did that together. He turned to Papa for the blessing over the wine. After that we each had piece of challah, torn off of the huge loaf. It had raisins in it. And we each sipped from a glass of wine - even the kids.

It was a wonderful dinner. First the servants served each of us gefilte fish. On the plate with the fish were slices of carrots cut into small Jewish stars. A dab of red horseradish was on each plate. Then the servants brought a large bowl with a lid in the shape of a hen sitting on her nest of eggs. From the bowl they served a delicious chicken soup with kreplach filled with ground meat. After that came the main dish, beef brisket. The servants passed around platters and we could each take as much as we wanted. With the brisket they passed a steaming bowl with a mixture of bow-tie noodles and kasha. When Mama made it she called it kasha varnishkes. There was also a sweet tzimmis with carrots and little dumplings. And for desert, there was a delicious cake made of almond paste.

Mama told Maish's mother it was a wonderful meal.

"Oh, it's just our usual Friday night dinner," she said.

"I thought perhaps it was a special occasion," said Papa.

"It is always special to share a good meal with family," said Maish's father. "But I do have some special good news to share with you."

Maish's father stood up. "As you know things have been bad here. The strikes have been very troubling to my business. So I've sold my leather factory. I'm also selling this house. I'm moving my family to Chicago." Maish's brothers and sisters cheered. His mother had a big smile.

"We want to be settled there before the baby is born," she said.

"Mazel Tov, congratulations," said Mama.

"Mazel Tov!" we all called out.

"What will you do there?" said Papa.

"I've asked my brother to find a store for me. I'll sell leather goods. Coats and jackets, wallets, purses, suitcases. I'll buy them from my friends here and I'll sell them at a good profit in America."

There was an awkward silence. Papa looked sad. Mama seemed to be waiting for him to say something. I could see tears starting in her eyes.

I grabbed a glass of water and said, "A toast. A toast to the new baby and to the Krupnicks in America. L' Chaim, to life."

"L' Chaim!" everybody shouted.

We were all quiet on the long walk home. I could hear Mama crying softly. Dvoira put her arm around Sarah. Papa seemed to be praying silently.

At home Dvoira said to Mama, "How long will it be before we have enough for our family to go?"

"Who knows," said Mama. "Maybe two years, maybe longer. And who knows what will happen in that time?"

The next day was Shabbos. Dvoira left early for a meeting. Before she left she whispered to me that she was going to ask if the people in the movement could help us to get to America like they had helped Anna, Avram and Dunya. Sarah and I were waiting when she came back.

"They can't help," she said. "They hardly have money to help their own members who get in trouble with the police. I guess we'll just have to wait for Kate and Anna to send enough money. With the little money I bring from the bagel bakery and the nuts and berries and mushrooms you two gather maybe we'll have enough in two years."

"I'm old enough to get a job in the bagel bakery," said Sarah. "Then I could help too."

"Don't even think of it," said Dvoira. "Papa wouldn't let you.

And if he did, I wouldn't. I've seen what happens to the youngest ones. The work is too hard and they get sick and sometimes they never get better."

Sarah and I promised to work harder to gather stuff from the woods to sell.

That night I fell asleep trying to think of ways I could help get the money. I had a strange dream.

The Czar's soldiers came in the night and dragged me out of my bed and said I was the oldest son of a Jewish family so they were taking me to the army. My Papa shouted that they don't have the right to do that anymore. The soldiers just laughed at him. The next thing in my dream, I was wearing a uniform which was way too big for me and marching up and down a field with a bunch of other Jewish boys my own age. There were men on horses who kept us marching up and down and hit us if we fell behind. Then we had to march for a long time with heavy packs on our backs. In the dream we never seemed to get anywhere. We just marched and marched. If we stopped or fell down, someone came with a stick and hit us and made us get up. In my dream I missed my family and cried a lot.

I woke up early the next morning and was glad my dream was over but I was still shaking all over from the memory of the dream. I lay there for a while and an idea came to me for how we could get the money for our trip.

Dvoira had already gone to her job at the bagel bakery. Mama was out delivering her milk and Papa was finishing his morning prayers. I told Sarah that when Mama came home I was going to see Dvoira about an idea I had. She said she would come with me.

I told Mama we wanted to go see Dvoira but I didn't tell her my idea. Mama gave us some cheese and bread to take along to eat for our lunch and made us promise to be back before dark. As we walked along we didn't say much. In the spring, flowers come up along the shore of the lake and grow in the grass along the road. Birds were flying among the trees in the woods and singing pretty songs. I was thinking that we lived in a beautiful place and that it was sad that we would be leaving soon. Sarah must have been thinking the same thing because she said, "Do you think there are pretty places like this in America?"

"I bet there are even prettier places there," I said.

When we got to the bagel bakery we had to wait a while for Dvoira to have a break. She came out and we sat down under a tree and I told her my idea.

"I dreamed last night the soldiers came and took me away to be in the army. It was a really bad dream but when I woke up I got the idea that Cousin Velvel could help us get the money to go to America."

"Cousin Velvel?" said Sarah "But he's way off some place in the woods. How could we even find him to ask him to help?"

"I think Dvoira can get a message to him," I said. "Can you Dvoira?"

"Honestly, I don't know," she said. "I could try to get a message to him. But I can't just ask him for money."

"No. Send the message that we want to thank him for the chickens he sent. Maybe he'll come to see us then," I said.

"It's worth trying," said Dvoira.

Friday night when Dvoira came home she told me that she sent the message to Cousin Velvel but she had no way of knowing whether he got it or not.

The next day, on Shabbos, when Papa came home from the shul

he had a man with him. It wasn't unusual for Papa to bring home a traveler who came to pray in the shul on Shabbos. He said, "I've brought a guest with me to share our meal." The man with him still had his talis, his prayer shawl, over his head. When he got into our house and the door was closed, he took off the prayer shawl.

It was Cousin Velvel. He hugged Papa and kissed him on both cheeks. Mama turned pale, "I still can't believe you're alive. The family was sure you were dead," she said.

"And I feel like I've come back from the dead," he said, and he hugged Mama too. Then he told the story again of how he was taken away when he was 14 and how he got to be a Captain by being a hard working soldier.

As we sat down for lunch, Cousin Velvel said, "So why did you send for me? Surely it wasn't to thank me for a few chickens?"

"The chickens were a wonderful gift," Papa said. "But we didn't send for you."

"I sent a message to you," said Dvoira. "It was Duvid Mendel's idea."

Everybody looked at me. I felt very small.

"Cousin - Captain Gutinsky," I said. "I was hoping you could help our family."

"I have a new name now," he said. "People are calling me 'the Wolf.' But you may call me Cousin Velvel. It feels very good to be with my family and to hear my Jewish name."

Papa looked very angry. "Duvid Mendel, You had no right to disturb our cousin. You should have asked me!"

"Never mind, Yankle Laib," said Cousin Velvel. "Let this clever boy tell me how I can help. I have no family of my own. I want to help if I can."

I explained about how we needed to get to America and it would take too long for us to have enough to pay for our tickets. "If you could help us," I said, "we could pay you back with the money we earn in America."

Now it was Mama who was mad at me. "I'm sorry, dear cousin," said Mama. "We don't need your help. In a year or two we'll have enough ourselves. The boy is just being impatient."

"My sister Kate in Chicago is having a baby in the summer. Mama is sad that she can't be there when the baby is born," said Sarah.

"And she will be there!" said Cousin Velvel. "All of you will be there. There is a certain travel agent in Vilna named Chaim Leiberman. Send word to him when you want to leave and he will arrange for your travel. I'll take care of your expenses and there is no need to pay me back. You can use the money you have saved to get settled in Chicago."

Mama burst into tears. "Thank you, but we couldn't take your money. It isn't right for my son to ask such a thing."

"These are terrible times and they will get worse," said Cousin Velvel. "It will give me great pleasure to help your family to be safe and together in America. I was torn from my family while I was still a boy. Please, let me help my cousins to be together now."

Papa had a funny look. "Excuse me, Velvel, but I need to ask - how did you come by this money?"

Cousin Velvel laughed so hard he started coughing.

"Call it back pay from the Czar, for my years of loyal service. All that I've taken from the Czar and his army is far less than he owes me. One day all of Russia will take back what he owes each of us," he said.

Mama stood up and walked over to where Cousin Velvel was sitting. She kissed him on the forehead and said, "Thank you, thank you. In spite of all they did to you, you kept your kind heart and your Jewish soul."

"Cousin Velvel," I said, "come with us. You can start a new life in America too."

"No, Duvid Mendel," he answered, "I have work to do here. The Czar made me into a soldier. I'm a good one. It's all I know how to do. Now I can use what I learned to free my people."

The next two weeks were like a whirlwind had struck our family. And the whirlwind was Mama. She took charge of everything. She decided we needed two weeks to get ready to leave and not one day more. Papa must go to Vilna on Monday morning to meet with Mr. Lieberman and take care of train and boat tickets. While he was in Vilna he was to send something called a telegram to Kate and Anna telling them we were coming and when and where we would arrive.

Telegrams must go very fast, because by the end of the week Dvoira brought a telegram that had come for us from Kate. Maish would meet our boat in New York to make sure we got through the place called Ellis Island where all the people like us coming into America were brought. Then Maish would take us on the train to Chicago and we all would be together again.

For the first week Dvoira still worked at her job in the bagel bakery. Then it was her job to go into Smorgon and buy the food and other things we would need for our trip to America. The ship we would be traveling on was supposed to have kosher food for the Jewish passengers but Papa and Mama didn't trust that so we would carry our own food for the whole trip.

By Thursday, market day, Mama had decided what few things

we could take with us. That wasn't hard because we didn't have much worth taking anyway. Each of us picked out our best clothes. The rest went to the committee that gives clothes to poor people. They'd have to be pretty poor to want our old clothes, I thought to myself.

Mama had Sarah and me take a few things from our house like furniture, dishes, pictures, and vases to friends and neighbors. We took everything else to the market on Thursday and Sarah and I had the job of selling it. Mama wrote a list of prices for everything. But Sarah and I let people bargain with us. I was pretty good at that. I even got more than Mama wanted for a few things.

Besides organizing us all for what needed to be done, Mama cleaned the house. Oi, did she clean the house. Everything had to be scrubbed. The dirt floor had to be swept and fresh sand sprinkled over it. The walls and shelves had to be scoured. The yard had to be swept and every bit of trash thrown away. The house wasn't really ours. It belonged to the shul. Nobody would be living there for a while. One of the farmers would act as the rabbi when Papa was gone. They hoped they would find a young rabbi to come, but that might take time. Still, Mama had to leave the house as clean as she could get it.

I decided I would go to say goodbye to Vanya. I didn't want to just go to his house and knock on the door. So I waited a little ways down the street until I saw him come out. He was walking away from where I was hiding, so I quietly came up behind him put my hands over his eyes and said, "Guess who?"

"Duvid Mendel," he said.

"How did you know?" I said.

"First, of all," Vanya said, "I told you you're not the only smart kid in Smorgon. Second, I heard you were moving to America so I was expecting you to come to say goodbye. And third, nobody in the world sounds like you when they say 'guess who?' in Belarussian."

There's an oak tree in the main square in Smorgon and Vanya and I climbed up into it. "So why is your family going to America?" he said. I told him about Kate's baby. I left out the part about Cousin Velvel. But a little while later he said, "Have you heard about the man they call 'The Wolf' who has a camp in the woods and who is making trouble for the Czar's army? You think maybe that's your father's cousin who saved our sisters from being sent to Siberia?"

I didn't say anything.

"I guess if you knew that you wouldn't tell anybody," he said.

"You're right. If I knew whether Cousin Velvel was the Wolf I wouldn't tell anybody," I said.

"Fair enough," he said.

We didn't say anything for a couple of minutes. And then he said, "My family might not stay in Smorgon very long either. Since Dunya left there are people always following Papa when he leaves the church."

"Have you heard from Dunya since she left?" I asked.

"She sends letters but Papa won't let us open them," he said. "He loved Dunya so much but now it's like she's dead. He won't forgive her for marrying Avram."

I shook my head and Vanya changed the subject. "So what will you do in America? Will you become a rabbi like your father?"

"In America," I said, "I will go to school, I will learn everything I can and I will get rich. If you're smart in America it's easy to get rich. And will you become a priest like your father?"

"Not a chance," said Vanya. "My father is a good man. He really cares about people. But things will get worse around here. When I'm old enough, I may find The Wolf and join his rebels to fight the Czar."

When we climbed down from the tree he said, "Tag, you're it," and I chased him around the square and when I caught him we wrestled a while. We got up finally and shook hands and I said, "I'll write to you."

He said, "Yeah? In what language?"

"I guess it will be English," I said, and we both laughed, shook hands once more, and went off in different directions.

That night there was a soft knock on the door. When I opened it there was Vanya's mother looking very nervous and sad.

"Is your mother at home?" she said. "I'd like to see her."

I called Mama. She put down her broom and dusted herself off and came to the door.

"Good evening," she said. "Please come in."

"If it's all right with you," she said, "could we talk out here, privately? It will only take a few minutes."

"Of course," Mama answered, and she went out and closed the door.

I listened and I could make out their voices with the door closed but not what they were saying. I thought I heard Dunya's mother crying. After a few minutes Mama came in alone. She had an envelope which she stuffed in the top of her dress. "Poor woman," she said. "She misses her daughter but her stubborn husband won't let her stay in touch with Dunya."

We knew that Dunya and Avram had been married by the ship's captain and were living near Anna and that she and Anna were working in the same sweat shop making ladies clothes. Avram was working for an animal doctor and was going to go to school to learn more about animals.

A little while later there was another knock on the door. When I opened it there didn't seem to be anyone there. But then I heard a man's voice. It was Father Vasily standing in the shadows. "I'd like to speak to the Rabbi," he said. "Please ask him to come out."

Papa heard him and went out to talk to Father Vasily. They must have walked away because I couldn't hear their voices.

"Father Vasily is leaving Smorgon," Papa said when he came back. "He is being moved to a church in Minsk. He's had too much trouble with the police here. He wanted us to get word to Dunya that the family was moving and how to reach them. I don't think he has forgiven her for marrying a Jew but if she writes to her mother he won't interfere anymore."

Mama showed him the letter Dunya's mother had given her to take to Dunya.

Dvoira said, "See Papa, times are changing for all of us."

"Times are changing," said Papa. "But these changes are hard for all of us. For me and for Father Vasily, the changes may be too much for us to bear."

Our last Shabbos in Karka was really special. Friday night every seat in the shul was full. Papa looked very sad during the evening but when he got up to speak he seemed very calm. He spoke about how Jews in all of history had been forced to wander from place to place when things got bad for them. And he talked about how Jews continued to live their lives as religious Jews obeying the laws written in the Torah and Talmud. Then he talked about how his daughters and their friends believed that the day was coming when Jews no longer had to live apart from others and they could be full citizens of the countries they lived in. In America, they said, Jews already have such rights.

"But when Jews have such rights would they continue to live their lives as Jews? I don't have the answer to this question," Papa said.

Saturday night was even more special. The Havdalah service was like a party. Even the other Rabbis from Smorgon came. A lot of wine was drunk. Our neighbors brought food to share and small gifts for our family. The rabbis gave Papa a beautiful copy of the Torah bound in leather with gold Hebrew letters on the cover.

Everybody wished us a happy and prosperous life in America.

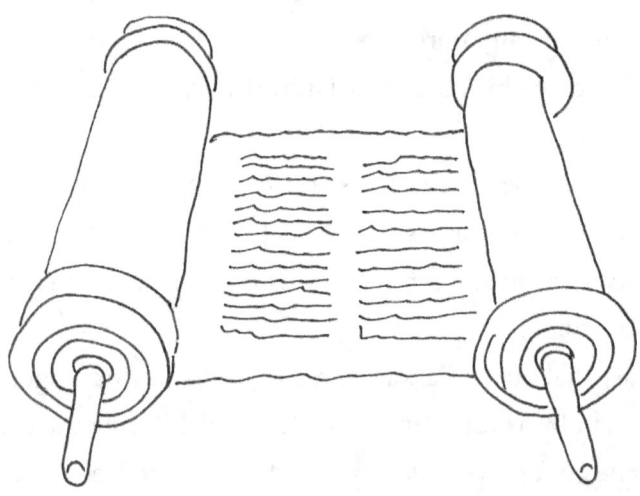

And so here we sit on the train platform in Smorgon waiting to start our journey by train and by ship to America. But Papa isn't sitting. He keeps pacing up and down, muttering to himself.

"Papa," I say "What's the good of worrying about what will happen to us in America? If we live, we'll see."

www.ingramcontent.com/pod-product-compliance
Lightning Source LLC
Chambersburg PA
CBHW052035070526
44584CB00016B/2051